Mexico
BLUE-RIBBON
Fly Fishing Guide

Largemouth Bass to Big Game

KEN HANLEY

Mexico

BLUE-RIBBON

Fly Fishing Guide

Largemouth Bass to Big Game

KEN HANLEY

Frank Amato

PORTLAND

Acknowledgments

Taking an assignment centered on my home waters is demanding enough—but tackling a whole country was quite another proposition! This project wouldn't be complete without the substantial network and assistance of friends who contributed their valuable skills and knowledge.

To me, the project represents a real celebration of kindred spirits. It showcases a passion for travel, a passion for fly fishing, and a passion for evolving.

I'd like to take this opportunity to thank the people who became "Team Mexico."

The exquisite flies tied for this project were provided by Mark Hoeser, Andy Burk, Jay Murakoshi, Del Brown, and Jeff Yamagata. As fly designers, and master tiers, their impressive skills bring a practical beauty to the world of fly fishing.

Many of the slides came from the talents of Glenn Kishi, Ralph and Lisa Cutter, John Shewey, Ray Beadle, Dan Blanton, Rick Martin, Jeff Solis, and Terry Gunn. Their sumptuous images bring a realism to "the Mexico experience."

As a student of fly fishing, I'm constantly seeking information on tackle, technique, and the natural history of game fish. Special thanks go to Ray Beadle and Howard McKinney for their gracious (and enthusiastic) sharing of rigging skills, as well as blue water and tarpon knowledge respectively.

I'd also like to acknowledge my colleagues in the travel industry (too numerous to list). Their understanding of the travel market was essential to this project.

Dedication

Cheers to pioneers past, and the future adventurers
who'll expand our fly-fishing arena.

Books by Ken Hanley

California Fly Tying & Fishing Guide
Surf Zone, Fly Fishing Afoot
Western Bass, Fly Fishing Afoot
The No Nonsense Guide to Fly Fishing In Northern California

©1999 by Ken Hanley

All inquiries should be addressed to:
Frank Amato Publications, Inc.
P.O. Box 82112 · Portland, Oregon 97282 · 503-653-8108

Cover Photo: Rick E. Martin
Back Cover Photo: Dan Blanton
Interior photographs by Ken Hanley unless otherwise noted.
Book Design: Amy Tomlinson

Printed in Canada
1 3 5 7 9 10 8 6 4 2

ISBN: 1-57188-154-9   UPC: 0-66066-00352-2

Table of CONTENTS

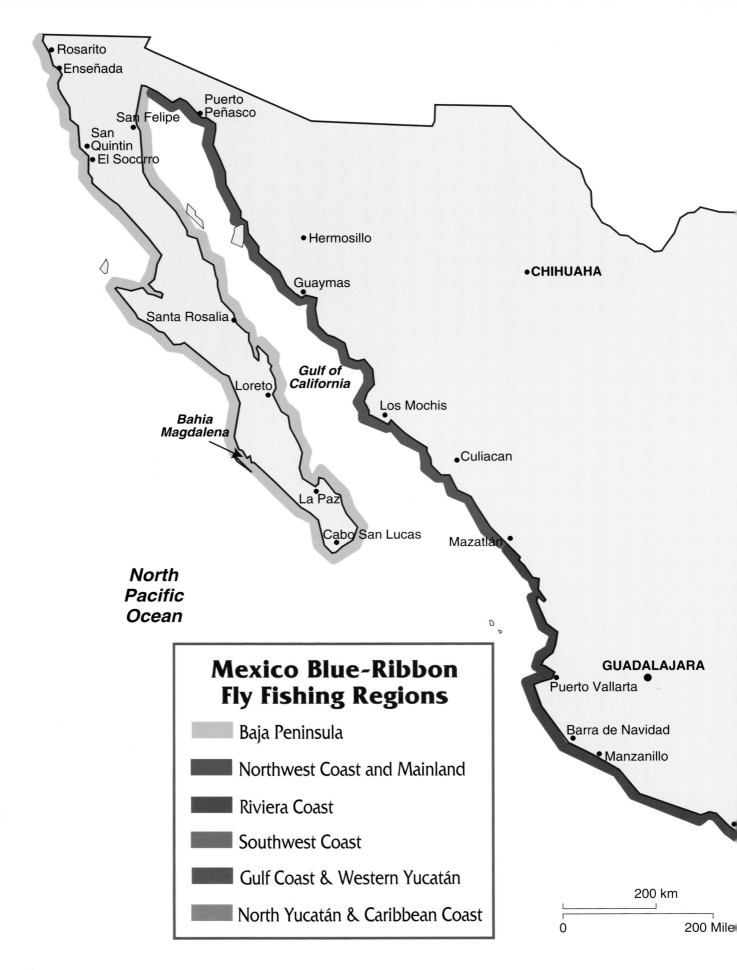

North Pacific Ocean

Mexico Blue-Ribbon Fly Fishing Regions

- Baja Peninsula
- Northwest Coast and Mainland
- Riviera Coast
- Southwest Coast
- Gulf Coast & Western Yucatán
- North Yucatán & Caribbean Coast

Rosarito
Enseñada
San Felipe
Puerto Peñasco
San Quintin
El Socorro
Hermosillo
CHIHUAHA
Guaymas
Santa Rosalia
Gulf of California
Loreto
Los Mochis
Bahia Magdalena
Culiacan
La Paz
Cabo San Lucas
Mazatlán
GUADALAJARA
Puerto Vallarta
Barra de Navidad
Manzanillo

200 km

0   200 Mile

Foreword

Dan Blanton

Ken has been a good friend and colleague for many years. The first time we worked together, teaching a basic saltwater fly fishing clinic for a local pro shop, I was extremely impressed by his inexhaustible energy. Ken exudes excitement and incredible enthusiasm for his subject. His energy is immediately transferred to his students. He heightens their spirit of adventure, leaving them with an incredible urge to get out and do it! Ken conveys his knowledge with sincerity, a light heart, a great sense of humor, and marvelous presentation and timing—he is a combination teacher and entertainer. It works.

I've followed Ken's writings for over a decade and he is always right on. He does his research and gives credit where credit is due. He is a writer true to his word. Ken is also a skilled fly fisher with a broad spectrum of experience ranging from panfish to saltwater. Fly fishing Mexico is his forte and it comes through in this book.

If there is one commonality he and I share, it is a love for Mexico and the incredible fly fishing it offers. I have always been enamored with Mexico and Central America. I particularly enjoy the Baja and Yucatán regions. I first fished the Baja back in the 1960s, car-topping tin boats and camping on its beaches. Friends and I took countless varieties of marine critters on fly gear and logged many incredible experiences. Doing this took planning, preparation, and a huge spirit of adventure. Today, I still fish Mexico annually, but now opt to stay at various lodges and hotels, hiring panga guides or sportsfishers to take me to the hot bite. Mexico offers the fly fisher one of the best angling bargains available today. For me, the camping is over...

Mexico, especially the Baja, has proved to be one of the most important experiences in my long fly fishing career. Ken's book takes me back, it also causes me to look forward to new frontiers and other exciting fly fishing adventures. He has made it easy by doing all the leg work, and rekindling my own inherent spirit of adventure.

I have great faith in Ken, both as a writer and a fly fisher —and in this book. Job well done!

Chapter ONE

Introduction to the Country

Welcome to Campeche!

Somewhere back in elementary school I was officially introduced to "our neighbors to the south." You know the scenario; a world map hanging over the chalkboard, flags splashing color throughout the classroom, and the teacher playing snippets of Mariachi bands celebrating the joys of Cinco de Mayo. My classmates, many of whom were of Mexican descent, prepared a wonderful feast of exotic tastes and textures. The food was heaven to a kid who exhibited a penchant for spicy edibles. I mean to say, I bought into the whole enchilada! The Mexican experience seemed so vibrant, the land so mysterious, this was a place I wanted to know more about—for me, the introduction was magical.

Growing up in California exposed me to a cornucopia of the Mexican culture. Through childhood friends, and their immediate families, I was given a window to the intimate images of life down south. What a wonderfully rich tapestry it was to behold. It was in the mid-'60s that I actually got an opportunity to travel to this exquisite land. The wild Baja Peninsula held up to my fantasies. In fact, it was truly better. The initial impact of that high school biology trip kindled a fire that lasts to this day. It's a wanderlust spirit that now embodies my fly fishing passion. Mexico performs a siren's song, and fly fishing is but an instrument for me to revel in her refrain.

My travels south have taken me to hidden coves and atop steaming volcanoes. At various times the tools for exploration ranged from backpack and ice ax, to surfboard and fly rod. I've had my senses reel from the irresistible variety of environment and adventure. Each expedition provided answers and solutions, while at the same time prompting a new inquisitiveness within me. I simply needed to return for the next episode.

Nowadays, just about anyone you talk to knows of a friend that's traveled to Mexico. The country is one of the most frequented destinations for vacationing "Norte Americanos." And why not—the price is right, the place is exotic, and the locals are charming. It's a formula that generally matures into treasured memories for most tourists. Make no mistake about it, travel through this diverse landscape is a prize sought after by savvy pilgrims. Only recently has the fly fishing community begun to discover the wealth of opportunity across our mutual border.

Sport angling has a long established history in international waters. Though most of the experience has centered around conventional tackle, fly fishing is a relatively new pursuit around the Mexican countryside. The majority of what we've established down there has come in less than 25 years to date. However, for all the exploration and technique development we've enjoyed in recent times, we can trace our history to a select few who made the first explorations with a fly rod around the late fifties. Sometimes they were outrageous. Sometimes they were ingenious. They were always cutting edge, and definitely inspirational. These fly rod pioneers showcased to the world a luxuriant new frontier for "casting feathers."

I fancy this guide as much a travelogue, as it is a fishing text.

I've compiled valuable information covering everything from transit to housing. I believe to maximize your venture, you need to address the very basic needs of international travel. Along with this "tourist" data you'll gain insight into the natural history of Mexico's game fish and suggested fly tackle options.

Mexico is a country covered with mountains. The interior can be difficult and demanding for tourists. High barren deserts and thick humid jungles are both dominated by mountainous terrain. Resources for the international traveler can be nonexistent at times and, because of this potential barrier, much of the angling experience in this book has been directed toward coastal exposure.

Saltwater monopolizes the scene. Its easy access and unlimited potential keeps sport fishers engaged in year-round pursuits. The country offers thousands upon thousands of coastal miles for exploration. These same briny waters are teeming with exotic creatures. From the cold Pacific currents of Northern Baja, to the warm seas off of Quintana Roo, Mexico serves up an amazing range of species and habitats.

I've arranged the book to divide the saltwater experience into five distinctive categories: surf zone, estuary and flats, rocky shore and kelp beds, inshore, and offshore waters. Fly fishers on foot, or working from small skiffs and kayaks, even those heading out in muscle cruisers will find information to help them hook-up in the salt.

Freshwater fly fishers don't fret—there's an ever expanding world-class fishery among the reservoirs of the mainland. Largemouth bass reign supreme in these waters. They routinely grow to exhibit impressive strength and size. The fishery is virtually untapped. Fly rodders can count on the quality of the experience.

Trout aficionados can even find game in the canyons and arroyos of Baja's Sierra San Pedro Martir. The journey is a step back in time with a sublime sense of adventure.

Though the text covers classic destinations, the project expands to include numerous little-known gems. It's my hope that this guide will enlighten and enhance your fly fishing quest. To experience Mexico for the first time, is to grab hold of a comet's tail. The ride is phenomenal and the memories are bright. Don't be surprised if the adventure ignites a desire to return. . . the place creates a pure fly fishing addiction!

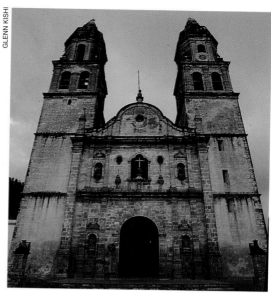

The heart and soul of Mexico.

Stronghold against pirate raids in the Gulf.

Chapter TWO

General Travel Logistics

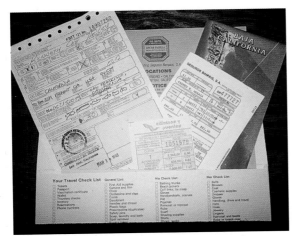

Acquire the correct documents before you travel.

You can take a commercial flight down. You can drive your own car down. You can sail with friends, or even participate on a cruise line to experience the wonderful fly fishing of Mexico. There is no other international angling destination so easily accessed, offering such diverse and rich opportunities. The game fish are abundant and the settings are mind boggling. There's an entire country to explore south of our border, and few have ventured "off the beaten path" with a fly rod in hand.

One of the beauties of traveling to Mexico is that it offers solid action on a year-round basis. There's literally a hot bite to be found during every month of the year. In order to tap into this treasure chest you'll need to prepare yourself before venturing off. A well versed traveler enjoys the advantage of fine-tuning their schedule (and resources) to maximize their angling endeavors. Pre-trip planning is key. It will make your excursion as stress-free as possible. (At the end of this chapter we'll supply you with a list of resources to ease your travel plans.)

Tourists wishing to enter the country need to address permits and other legal matters first. The best advice I can give you is to contact one of the Mexican government tourism offices for the latest information. Another valuable resource is any travel agent that specializes in the region. Not all agents are created equal—it pays to shop a bit before you commit to working with any single agency.

You'll find that a tourist card is required for most trips. If you plan on traveling to only the border towns along Mexico Highway 1 and Highway 5, you won't need a card if your stay is less than 72 hours in length. If you need to travel farther into the country, you can obtain either a single-entry (valid for 90 days) or a multiple-entry (valid for 180 days) to fit your specific needs. Tourist cards are free and you'll automatically receive one if you book a flight or cruise line into Mexico.

In addition to a tourist card you'll be required to carry "proof of citizenship." Most travelers

Do-it-yourself travelers have plenty of lodging options.

bring along a copy of their birth certificate or a passport. Other documents that would validate who you are could include voter registration, an affidavit of citizenship, or a military ID if applicable.

Anyone operating a land vehicle will need a current driver's license and Mexican auto insurance. All vehicles traveling through the country's mainland must be registered for a permit prior to entry. There's no fee to obtain such a permit. Baja travelers are exempt from this requirement. To eliminate some of the legal restrictions, you might want to consider renting a vehicle after you enter the country (via airport, etc.). Rentals are an excellent way to maximize your angling access. You can take care of all the necessary arrangements prior to leaving the states. There will be more information covering land vehicles and rentals in the following chapter.

Sportsfishing licenses are required no matter where you fish. Mexico is no exception to this rule. I'm sure you'll run across plenty of anglers who don't bother to secure a license, but hey, that doesn't make it right. Unlike the hefty fees of some famous destinations, Mexican Sportsfishing Licenses are a genuine bargain. There's no price differential between freshwater or saltwater venues. As of this printing, you have three options to apply for; one week ($12.95), one month ($19.00), or an annual permit (for just $25.30). Heck, that's cheaper than a resident license in my own state!

In each of the upcoming regional chapters you'll find specific details concerning transportation options, lodging, and other support services. Whether you opt for a prepackaged program, or prefer the "do-it-yourself" approach, you'll find Mexico can meet your needs at any level. When you're booking your adventure, be aware of the tourist season in which you wish to travel. Peak season (from November to May) often demands higher rates. Before we delve into each region I'd like to present you with some generic advice concerning airfare, accommodations, camping, and the Information Hotline.

Air travel south of the border is well developed throughout most of the country. There isn't a sector you can't reach by using some major international carrier or one of Mexico's in-country services. Some of the international carriers include Alaska Airlines, American West, Delta, United Airlines, Mexicana, and Aeromexico. Keep an eye peeled for the constant fare wars taking place. Promotional fares, often referred to as APEX Tickets, can be a great savings if you can live with the restrictions placed on the purchase. Personally I don't find the restrictions annoyingly prohibitive.

If you're tempted to do business with a consolidator or discount club, beware of scams. I'm not saying they're all scam artists. What I am saying is scam artists can often find this arena profitable. If you aren't sure of the provider you can always check directly with the airline, or contact The U.S. Department of Transportation's Office of Consumer Affairs (telephone; 202-366-2220). There's tremendous savings to be had—and unsuspecting victims to be had—so when in doubt pay the extra expense for security and peace of mind.

The gateway airports include; Acapulco, Cancún, Cozumel, Guadalajara, Hermosillo, Ixtapa, Loreto, Mazatlán, Mérida, Mexico City, Puerto Vallarta, San José (Los Cabos), and Tijuana. Each of these hubs can provide direct flights to, and from, Mexico. Secondary airports en route, still significant in angling terms, are; Ciudad Obregon, Huatulco, La Paz, Los Mochis, Puerto Escondido, Tampico, and Veracruz. As I mentioned earlier, you can travel to any part of the country by plane if you so desire.

When it comes to lodging the game is wide open. You can opt for the posh setup of a Club Med, or park yourself under a thatched-hut

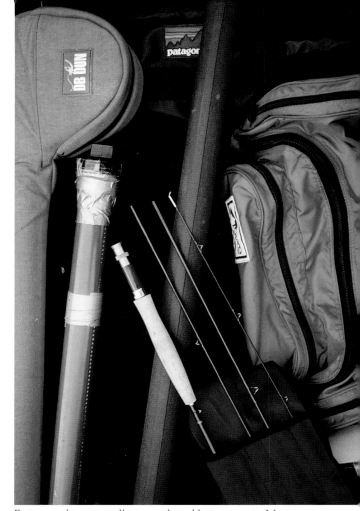

Be prepared to carry all you need, tackle is sparse in Mexico.

Campers at Punta Chivato.

cabaña. Vacation packages abound in the land down south. You can tailor your housing to any standard you please. Hotels are typically the category of full-service modern facilities. They represent the higher end of the market. Prices will likely start around $100 based on two people/per night. Motels and guest houses are moderately priced, yet often provide high-quality service. The price range is $50 to $90. These facilities are generally not as expansive as at a hotel. The next level of housing is "budget," and it can be pretty basic. For many travelers, as long as they're dry in the monsoons, or semi-cool during a heat wave, budget inns can help stretch their vacation dollar. Consider $35 to $50 reasonable for this category.

As for dedicated angling lodges, they are still few and far between. Searching countrywide you'd be hard pressed to find more than a dozen. Unlike Alaska where a mountain-styled lodge is the norm, it's indicative of Mexico to provide a villa-like atmosphere instead. Specialty facilities can offer you the most detailed services for an angling vacation. The standards for these accommodations are extremely high. Their locations are always prime and they provide all the support services you'll need. You pay for the extra quality but it's well worth the investment. This may be even more of an issue if your travel plans are confined to a shorter schedule. Without the luxury of a few days to burn, while you investigate regional waters, "short timers" need to tip the odds right from the get go. That's usually accomplished by taking advantage of the custom services provided at an angler's villa. I've come to the conclusion that sometimes you just have to cut loose with the pesos—know what I mean. Prices will begin around $150 per day. Fly fishing oriented facilities are becoming much more available as the sport continues to expand in popularity.

Those of you who want to "dirt-bag it" (and I say that affectionately from one adventure junky to another) can camp to your heart's content. There's semi-developed facilities in a few national parks, and numerous commercial sites along village waterfronts. You can pretty much establish a campsite anywhere you find empty beaches and dunes. How can this be you ask? It's simple, all beaches are seen as part of the public domain by the Mexican government.

Now that I've made that sweeping statement, there are still a few exceptions to the rule. Some commercial developments hold access rights to a beachhead. They aren't required to grant the public any access through their property. If you can find a way around their holdings you still have the right to use the beach itself. Another exception to the rule might be community-owned property known as ejidos. You can usually gain permission by asking who in the village might control the access rights. If you're asked by authorities to leave the premises, by all means pack up and move. There's plenty of space down south and you'll surely find another suitable site in a short time. I have never experienced a negative encounter (thievery, bullies, etc.) yet I don't advertise any vulnerability. Listen to that gut feeling and let it guide you to a safe location. Common sense and good judgment should be "standard equipment" when you participate in the camping scene.

The availability of commercial camping facilities spans the full gambit in Mexico. You could pay as little as $3 per night but don't expect that from a resort-operated site. Slick, tightly run, full-service operations are the exception more often than not. Smaller, less sophisticated operations are more the norm. Most sites will provide you with bathrooms and hot showers. Restaurants and groceries are often nearby.

Another option, freewheeling, is the network of RV and trailer parks throughout the country (particularly on the Baja Peninsula). This resource is one of the best buys in-country. The facilities are generally very clean and secure. The multiple services they can provide you are a welcome relief at times. You can't beat this system for easing your travels and keeping you rolling! By the way, you don't need an RV to participate here, tent camping is welcome at most of the locations. Fees are similar to what you pay here at home. They typically range from $15 to $40 per site.

There's an added bonus from participating within this system. Anglers trailering skiffs and runabouts are the best resource for hot-bite information. The angling community as a whole is very supportive of each other. I've frequently been a satisfied participant in this information hotline. I'm sure it will rapidly become another tool for your success. The hotline can help you narrow down the overwhelming array of options as you explore the countryside with fly rod in hand.

I'd like to focus once more on the safety of traveling through Mexico. It's no worse than your hometown and in some cases much better. Sure there's some crime. You don't have to be a part of that. Travel smart and stay sharp. In my opinion, anybody who tempts fate with stupidity gets what they deserve. I realize this is a bit harsh, but in reality it's not that difficult to have a safe, enjoyable trip. The only times I've ever been vandalized have been on the Russian River and Putah Creek in Northern California!

GENERAL TRAVEL RESOURCE LIST

Mexican Government Tourism Office (Western U.S.)
10100 Santa Monica Blvd., suite #224
Los Angeles, CA 90067

Mexican Government Tourism Office (Eastern U.S.)
405 Park Avenue, suite #1401
New York, NY 10022

Stop by any U.S. Passport Office and request the latest Consular Information Sheets (prepared by the U.S. Department of State's "Overseas Citizen's Emergency Center").

These briefs cover such subjects as security, politics, health issues, embassy locations, etc. The documents can provide critical information if you plan on touring in the backcountry.

Mexico Department of Fisheries
2550 5th Avenue, suite #101
San Diego, CA 92103
(licenses and regulations)

Aeromedevac
6340 Riverdale Street
San Diego, CA 92120
(24 hour worldwide emergency air ambulance service. Carry these emergency numbers with you, toll free in Mexico 95-800-832-5087, from the U.S. 1-800-462-0911)

One of the many full-service lodges available.

RALPH CUTTER

Chapter THREE
Weather and Roads

This is a huge country with plenty of variation when it comes to climate. Most tourists conjure cozy images of balmy breezes and swaying palm trees, or bright sun-drenched beaches with serene surf. This certainly can be the reality if you pay attention to both regional and seasonal patterns. On the other hand, travelers expecting this paradise to wrap them in tranquility 365 days a year just aren't being realistic. You could get the surprise of a lifetime if a tropical storm front comes blasting over the countryside. Again, pre-trip planning and an eye for fine-tuning while you're afield can make all the difference in the world. Learning to ask the right questions is really what it takes. It begins with acquiring some basic background information on seasons and regions. This book's layout incorporates five primary sectors: Northwest Coast and Mainland, Riviera and Southwest Coast, Gulf Coast and Western Yucatán, Northern Yucatán and Caribbean Coasts, and the Baja Peninsula.

First, looking at the country as a whole, October through May represents the dry season. The months of December, January, and February are most desirable. The wet season consists of June through September. The rainy months could exhibit frequent short-term showers, almost on a daily basis. The storms during this season can build to a torrential intensity. Hurricane season ordinarily occurs in the warmest months. Don't be alarmed, just be aware. Locally known as a chubasco, hurricane activity can occur along the Gulf, Yucatán and Caribbean coasts, or the Pacific Riviera and Southwest Coastal regions. That pretty much encompasses the majority of Mexico's coastline communities.

There's more to Mexican weather though than just wind and rain. The heat factor in Mexico can be downright brutal. Add to that a very high humidity rating in some cases, and the situation becomes less appealing for many tourists. Temperatures will fluctuate between habitat and elevation. Much of the winter season you'll experience temperatures in the mid-70s to high-80s. The summer months can range well above 90 degrees. I can remember a trip when the average temperature was 105 degrees with the hottest day recorded a mere 113! Of course actual temperature ratings depend specifically on where you'll be staying. A good example of this temperature differential would be Enseñada (northern Baja) and Cozumel (Caribbean Coast) during January. To the north you'll find lows in the 40s and highs to the mid-60s. Much farther south the temperature ratings could chart from the high-60s

Many towns have cobblestone or tiled streets.

into the 80s. As the saying goes, "know what you're getting into."

Remember Mexico's terrain varies from high desert plateau to coastal mangrove. There's even high-altitude summits covered with perpetual snowfields. With such extreme variations in environment we should continue to refine our climatic picture.

A closer portrait of the primary sectors would be as follows:

Northwest Coast and Mainland: Winter months are cool (50s to 60s). Summer months can be very hot (90+). Rainfall can be present year-round, though generally it's pretty sporadic.

Riviera and Southwest Coast: Winter months mild (tropical, 70s to 80s). Summer months can get very hot (90+). This is a high humidity region during the summer. Rainfall is definitely more frequent.

Gulf Coast and Western Yucatán: Winter months mild (tropical, 70s to 80s). Summer months hot and humid. Humidity can be stifling as you move away from the coastline. Northern winds crossing the Gulf of Mexico bring rainfall and cooler temps. The "Northerns" (Los Nortes) occur during the autumn and winter months.

Northern Yucatán and Caribbean Coasts: Generally pretty warm year-round (80s to 90s). With the help of those magnificent tradewinds, the thermometer is kept somewhat at bay. Expect periodic rainfall from late spring into autumn.

The Baja Peninsula: The Pacific side is likely to be cooler than the Sea of Cortez. The entire Baja is dominated by arid desert. Humidity is more of an issue along the "Cortez Coast." Winter months in the northern peninsula can be cool (50s to 60s). Summer months in the north can be very hot (90+). Winter in the southern peninsula is mild (60s to 70s). Summer months in the south can soar (100+).

One of the greatest impacts of weather is seen with road conditions. Those of you planning on trailering a boat, or using a private vehicle for transport, should have some foundation information about the road system and driving legalities.

The major arteries throughout the entire country are paved and heavily traveled. In large part, Mexico's mainland territories provide paved surfaces. I include both highways and city streets here when applicable. Baja's paved system is more apt to be confined to coastal routes. To date, the Peninsula's interior rarely sports such treatment.

On rural or remote routes the majority of the time you'll share the road with commercial truckers and other tourist vehicles. Don't expect to see wide generous roadways. Do expect to see plenty of soft shoulders and marginal safety lanes. It's a wise idea not to venture off into the night unless you're absolutely sure of the road conditions and the directions to your destination.

As a general rule of thumb, the more prominent the city, the more hectic the driving style of the locals. Like home, the hustle and bustle of mass humanity creates a difficult environment at best.

The roads of Mexico are in a constant state of disrepair. This is particularly true of the secondary roadways. Generally they're little more than a grated dirt surface. Count on these passages to live up to their namesake unimproved. Genuinely smooth rides are a fairy tale for the most part. Yet the system today is infinitely better than in bygone days. Most any style vehicle can now function along these routes. But be forewarned—the continuous washboard

Typical unimproved secondary roadway.

grating can be a kidney buster, and chuckholes and ruts are still the norm. Steep grades can add to the strain on your vehicle. If there's been any heavy rains you could find the road conditions impassable. Be prepared for the worst, and be happy with what you get if it's a negotiable route. I find it nearly impossible to rate the quality of these backroads. Everyone has a different tolerance level to be sure. One driver might find the route a nightmare. Another might find it fun. One thing is certain and that's any unimproved road is never a guaranteed passage. If possible, I never drive with only one access route in mind.

Don't let all this talk of road conditions stop you from driving down south. I still believe it's one of the most fulfilling ways to explore the country. Nothing can replace a sound game plan. Make the extra effort to prepare your vehicle for harsh conditions. Take the time to develop an appropriate emergency road/repair kit. Contact your insurance carrier (or Vagabundos del Mar Boat and Travel Club) for details concerning safety tips for touring the Mexican countryside.

Let's take a closer look at the legal documents necessary to bring your vehicle across the border. You must have proof of ownership in the car. Your normal registration document will be fine for

Be sure your vehicle is ready for remote travel.

Towns and villages are abundant along the coast.

this. When you apply for your Tourist Card, request that it be stamped as a vehicle permit as well. Mexican auto insurance is mandatory. International policies don't apply down here. It's to your advantage to secure the appropriate insurance in the U.S. before you enter Mexico. You could readily acquire Mexican insurance through any AAA Auto Club outlet, Sanborn's Mexico Insurance offices at the border crossings, or any Mexican consulate and tourist office.

Here's a quick note concerning fuel availability; the government controls all of it! Pemex petrol is the name of the game in Mexico. It's not the highest standard you'll ever come across but it is the only brand you get to work with. Nova is low octane, Extra (or Magna Sin) is unleaded, and diesel is also available. Keep in mind that you'll need cash to make most purchases. Working with pesos in this situation could stretch your travel budget.

As I mentioned in the previous chapter, renting a rig is a real possibility. If your motivation for this option is to save oodles of money don't get involved. The reasons to take this option are to cut down on legal documents, eliminate independent insurance costs, and save the wear-n-tear on your own rig. Depending on the actual style of rental, your daily fees could range from $40 upward to

$100+. The longer you rent a vehicle, the better the savings offered. If you split the cost with a couple of traveling companions it isn't all that bad. Another way to reduce costs is to arrange, and pay for, the rental before you leave home. In order to rent once you're in Mexico, you'll need your driver's license and a credit card. You may find some agencies require a minimum age limit. Twenty-five seems to be the magic number for most.

Rental companies working in Mexico will have a familiar ring to their names. International chains such as Hertz, Avis, and Budget conduct business in most hub cities and airports. Major hotels in the country could also help make arrangements at your request.

There was a time (from the mid-70s into the early-80s) that I co-led quite a few Baja expeditions. I was on contract with a college to conduct adventure recreation programming and Mexico was the perfect classroom for my students. The adventures were known as "Overlanding." Each expedition combined the travel experiences of caravaning and backpacking into remote terrain.

Driving huge maxi-vans, laden with enough field equipment for two weeks of survival in the backcountry, I became pretty road-savvy while touring The Baja. Many of the lessons gained on those fantastic excursions still work for me today.

Most recently my driving partner's been Gregg Jones, a true desert rat if ever there was one. His 3/4-ton pickup and full camper shell has become a fly fishing Shangri-La for us. The following outline is a compilation of our "road safety package."

- a complete first aid kit
- complete tool set (including duct tape)
- water (five-gallon minimum)
- gasoline container (five-gallon minimum)
- antifreeze, premixed with water (two one-gallon jugs)
- oil (four-quart minimum)
- brake fluid, power steering fluid
- fan belt set
- spark plug wires (at least two to match the longest in your set)
- water hose repair kit
- fuel and air filters
- spare tire (and pump: 12-volt style is preferred)
- can of "stop leak"
- set of tire chains for traction in soft sand
- shovel and pickax
- heavy-duty tow strap
- spot light (12-volt style preferred)
- standard flashlight
- bandanas (used as pre-filters at the gas pumps)
- reflection tarp
- 100 feet of emergency cord

Again, I encourage you to contact your insurance carrier or a travel club for more suggestions on safety gear.

For those of you trailering a boat, here are a few more tips for the journey. Completely inspect the trailer and tires prior to your vacation. Check for signs of corrosion and loose (or missing) parts. Once you've taken care of any suspect findings, the trailer should be in prime condition.

Traveling through Mexico is tough on trailers and the following maintenance tips are advised. Routinely check the frame and axle for integrity. If you have surge style brakes, they might well require adjusting during your expedition. Carry a spare tire specifically designed for your trailering needs. The sidewalls on standard auto tires are too thin. You'll need a "scissors jack" to properly handle the load of your trailer. If your trailer isn't equipped with bearing protectors, it would behoove you to install some.

In addition to the recommended "road safety package" for your vehicle, carry the following basic items for your trailering security.

- spare trailer tire
- scissors jack
- extra bearings, seals
- extra winch strap, extra utility tie-down strap
- extra safety chains for coupling
- extra lug nuts, spring bolts, etc.
- spare bulbs and fuses
- grease for packing bearings

A Final Note On Safety

Considering the potential extremes of Mexican weather patterns, it's incumbent upon you to take basic safety precautions. I believe one of the most important aspects of safety is being actively prepared. At the most basic level this would include making the proper travel arrangements, assembling appropriate clothing, and bringing along any emergency items (ie: medications, first aid kits, legal documents, etc.).

"Nuts-n-Bolts" Travel Resource List

Mexico Surface Tourism Office for U.S. and Canada
2707 N. Loop W., suite #440
Houston, TX 77008
(Specially developed to deal with the needs of land travel; private vehicle access, road conditions, etc.)

Vagabundos del Mar Boat and Travel Club

190 Main Street
Rio Vista, CA 94571
(Specialize in private vehicle access, trailering boats, permits/insurance, etc.)

Discover Baja Travel Club

3065 Claremont Drive
San Diego, CA 92117
(Peninsula specialists, permits/insurance, etc.)

Chapter FOUR

Species Overview

The sheer volume of species taking residence in Mexican waters is astonishing. With over 800 known varieties what a miraculous menagerie they create. With fly fishing tackle and field techniques becoming more sophisticated, the list of "fly-caught species" is ever expanding. Specific tackle options will be addressed in the following chapter. At this time I'd like to present some foundation data on individual species. Let's focus our attention on 22 of the most celebrated fly rod game fish in Mexico.

LARGEMOUTH BASS

Three varieties of bass proliferate in the waters of the mainland. Mexican northerns are indigenous to the area. Two introduced species include pure-strain Florida largemouths and a super hybrid consisting of Texas and Florida strains. All of Mexico's bass are fast growing, deep-bodied specimens. They exhibit superior strength in all weight classes.

Pargo Colorado from the Riviera Coast.

DAN BLANTON

Nick Curcione with a Baja cabrilla (circa 1979).

These fish are supremely built for ambushing prey. Their fin structure and powerful tail exhibit large surface areas which afford them tremendous, explosive strength. Lurking amongst a variety of cover, the largemouth positions itself to intercept prey. Consider the bass a "short strike" predator. They'll be less likely to travel any significant distance to chase prey.

Largemouth in these waters feed mainly on forage populations. Tilapia are a main resource, while bluegill and crappie contribute to the bass' sustenance. Crawdads and other miscellaneous foods complete the largemouth's diet.

Fall, winter, and spring are the best months for bass down south. Typically January begins the pre-spawn cycle. During May, June, and July, the night cycle is key to some awesome action.

CALICO BASS

Calicos can carry the moniker of "kings of the kelp beds." Found primarily on the Pacific coast, their preferred habitat is along rocky shorelines and kelp forests. These bass are a terrific shallow-water game fish. Concentrations of calicos can typically be found in depths of 40 feet or less. Often they can be seen actively feeding at less than 10 feet deep. Built very much like a freshwater bass these salty brawlers feed in a similar manner. Concentrate your efforts near structure and cover. Open water usually won't provide heavy action. Their diet consists of smaller fish and crustaceans.

These game fish are a resident species. Individual populations won't migrate any significant distance during the year. Calico bass are always available, with the peak months being June and July. A solid bite occurs from May through October, while the extended season spans April through December. Boaters will have a distinct advantage targeting these fish.

SAND BASS

Three types of "sandies" live down south; spotted, barred, and goldspotted sand bass. The spotted bass has the widest distribution in Mexican waters. You can find them along the Pacific coast and throughout the Sea of Cortez. Spotted bass are another great shallow-water species. They congregate over softer bottomed habitat. Like calicos, they tend to stay close to rocky cover. Spotted bass also frequent areas where eelgrass is prominent.

These game fish are an outstanding catch around quiet bay environments. Sand bass feed primarily on crustaceans and small baitfish. Spots are a viable year-round catch. Prime activity could take place from May through September. You can pursue them either afloat or afoot.

PARGO

Here is a bass-like species. The pargo Colorado is typical of the group. It is a feisty, rapacious fish that lives among reefs and rocky shorelines. Both the inshore and onshore fly fisher can target these great sportsfish. Though they hang around tough craggy cover, some other varieties of snapper can also be found cruising over shallow flats. Generally found in tropical seas, snapper thrive around the country.

The pargo Colorado is a robust species with jaws like a steel

Northern Baja barred surfperch.

vise. Canine teeth add to the arsenal of this highly effective predator. Whether it's crushing shells, or chasing baitfish, it doesn't matter because the snapper eats what (and when) it wants to! Slightly
more elongate than a typical bass, the Colorado can anchor itself
amongst the crevasses and caves of tropical habitats. Working
depths of up to 30 feet is extremely productive for fly rodders.

Pargo are an excellent species to target April through August.
The extended bite could occur from early spring into the autumn
months. Boaters and rockhoppers alike can find success with these
outstanding game fish.

SPOTTED CABRILLA

Cabrilla belong to the sea bass family. They are a hearty bunch to be
sure. "Bottom-hugging" best describes this particular species. They
share a common diet with other rock dwellers. Crustaceans play a
prime role in cabrillas' feeding behavior.

Spotted cabrilla are most commonly found in the Sea of Cortez.
Available on a year-round basis, peak months include July and
August. The peak action could last longer as you travel south.
Cabrilla can be found from March through November depending on
the region you target. Anyone can catch this species. Fly fishers on
foot can be very effective working from rocky outcroppings.

BARRED SURFPERCH

Surfperch are probably the most prolific game fish living within the

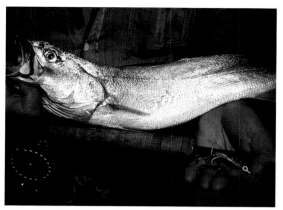

Northwest Coast corvina.

Baby tarpon from Western Yucatan.

surf zone itself. Barred perch reign supreme in Northern Baja's Pacific breakers. "Prince clowns" are an apt description for these scrappy runabouts. Their feeding signature is a series of rapidfire taps followed by a schizoid run. Their primary food source is the Pacific mole crab. They'll fulfill their dietary needs with shrimp, marine worms, softshell clams, and tiny baitfish if necessary.

The surfperch can be a highly mobile species. However, the majority of the local populations stay near a homebase beach. Barred perch frequently roam the surf zone in packs, and show a preference for sandy habitat.

You can venture for them during any month. Peak season is generally during the summer. An extended bite often takes place from March through August. Perch action will slow considerably once autumn is in full swing.

CORBINA

They're an ancient fish, and without question one of the toughest challenges for a fly fisher. The California corbina is a member of the

Rick Martin shows a beautiful Cabo roosterfish.

croaker clan. They have an elongate body sporting wide shoulders and a powerful broom-like tail. The most prominent feature concerning feeding behavior is the fish's inferior-positioned mouth. Their mouth is located completely on the underside of the head. A chin barbel is also present to aid the fish in locating its prey. Again, the Pacific mole crab is a preeminent food item. Mussels and soft-shell clams are other favored foods.

Corbina frequent the surf zone. You'll often find their backs exposed as they cruise the thin wash over a sandy beach. They roam in small groups or as solitary scouts.

The warm summer months are when you can expect to see these game fish active. The corbina's range in Mexico is confined to Northern Baja. To be precise, it's confined along the Pacific shoreline.

CORVINA

Here's a fish that's often mistaken for its cousin the Corbina. They are indeed both members of the same family, but there are instrumental differences between them (ie: mouth structure and dentures, diet, etc.). Three types of corvina are found in Mexican waters; the shortfin, the gulf, and the orangemouth. Using the short-fin corvina as our model, they have a pair of large canine teeth to help them trap prey. They feed heavily upon smaller fish, as well as a variety of crustaceans. Corvina live in a variety of shallow inshore habitat. They are particularly drawn to sandy niches.

Corvina are widespread in Mexico and available throughout the year. Peak season will vary from one region to the next. The Pacific bite is hot from November to February. It then appears to taper off, becoming almost non-existent during midsummer. The Cortez action can be sparse during winter, building into a solid bite from April through August. Boating or wading, any fly fisher can enjoy the corvina fishery.

SIERRA

They may not tip the scales at staggering weights but these are a hot game fish. As members of the mackerel and tuna family they're equipped for lightning fast speed. They favor open water as any true pelagic species would. Sierra roam near the surface in substantial schools. Living in the inshore environment they are especially prevalent just outside the breakers. They can also be found in bays, estuaries, and even in the surf line itself at times.

They come armed with a full set of needle-sharp teeth. They like to target baitfish, with sardines and anchovies at the top of the list. Baitfish populations usually dictate where the sierra will stay on the prowl.

Sierra are an accessible game fish throughout the year. During the winter you'll find them to be sporadic, fluctuating from red hot action to apparently disappearing overnight! Boaters have the edge in this game.

SNOOK

Here's another prime game fish with far reaching populations down south. Both the Pacific and Gulf regions offer great fare. While the Yucatán and Caribbean coast log-in with high action opportunities as well. You can count on this shallow-water species to live among lagoons, mangrove estuaries, open flats, and coastal rivers. At times, thick cover will help them establish potent ambush stations. Snook survive on baitfish, shrimp, and crabs.

Autumn and winter are both terrific time frames for pursuing snook. Because of their wide distribution, populations will show

Ray Beadle with a record Pacific Coast skipjack.

variations in peak periods. Snook are very temperature sensitive. If the water drops below 60 degrees the fish become far less aggressive. Boats are a real necessity to gain access to the coveted feeding grounds.

GREAT BARRACUDA

Make no mistake about it—Mexican barracuda are a pure feeding machine. This fine-tuned predator has exactly what it takes to run-down a host of food; a sleek hydrodynamic body, lots of teeth for ripping into prey, and a huge mouth to gulp down the remains. Their profile will remind you of a heat-seeking missile. Barracuda tend to school near the surface. Larger specimens are solitary predators.

The great barracuda roams open ocean and flats alike. The creature is on the hunt wherever easy prey exists. It's right at home prowling the edges of a mangrove habitat. If the situation calls for it, they could station themselves as steady as a rock. Their diet basically revolves around fish.

These large predators are common on the warmer coastlines. The Gulf of Mexico, plus the Yucatán and Caribbean coast, are major centers of action. They're available all year. Cooler water temperatures will tend to bring 'cuda onto the shallow flats in greater numbers.

PERMIT

This pompano is considered one of the top prizes on saltwater flats. They're also a cherished catch in the surf zone. Permit are a deep-bodied species. Their fin structure is built to complement erratic, slashing-style movements. The fish generally travel along channels and contours. As the tide builds and ultimately floods a flat, the permit will leave deeper water to hunt primarily for crabs. Their mouth is well designed to root for prey. The powerful jaws crush shells with ease.

Yucatan Peninsula snook.

Permit tend to school. However, you'll find plenty of solo acts cruising the flats. They appear to be in no hurry as they scour the bottom for crustaceans. Sight is a key factor in their feeding behavior. Oftentimes you'll find them "tail to the sky" working a specific patch of grass or sand.

The Yucatán and Caribbean regions play host to the largest populations of permit. It's a year-round adventure. September and October can offer outstanding action. January can be a peak month for the Yucatàn coast. Anglers on foot or in boats can pursue the great pompano.

BONEFISH

The ghost of the flats. That's their nickname and aptly so. Now you see them, now you don't! Their camouflage makes them extremely difficult to locate. That's especially important to their survival, as larger predators such as shark and barracuda dine on "bones."

The bonefish's diet essentially consists of crustaceans and mollusks. Other foods of lesser note include tiny fish, worms, and squid. Like the permit, bonefish are prone to root out their meals. Tailing fish are a sure sign of active feeders.

Another sign of foraging bones is known as "mudding." Puffs of disturbed marl are suspended, in essence creating a bonefish footprint at the surface.

Bonefish are the mini thoroughbreds of the shallows. Their signature is a scorching run when disturbed or caught. Boating and wading access can be equally effective depending on location.

Again, the Yucatán and Caribbean coasts offer the best angling. November and December are particularly good on the Caribbean side. Both coasts offer good action year-round.

TARPON

Simply put, tarpon are the undisputed heavyweights of the flats. These ancient warriors are seemingly built for battle. Huge scales and bony plates combine to give the fish an armour-like appearance. They're a high-flying, hard-driving adversary. These game fish aren't just found cruising the flats. Estuaries and large rivers are essential to the fish's life cycle. Both habitats play the duel roles of nursery and restaurant to the tarpon.

The "silver kings" target mullet and other baitfish as their favored foods. If tarpon are actively feeding you get signs of escaping bait, splashing and a genera raucous in the area. Typically they cruise the open water of shallow environments, but don't discount the productive habitat along mangrove snags.

Spawning appears to take place around the summer months. June through January offers excellent opportunities. October and November can be very solid. Angling is best found along the Gulf of Mexico, and of course the Yucatán/ Caribbean region. The use of boats gives an extreme advantage to access, and thorough exploration of tarpon terrain.

Ed Givens takes a rest after working in this wahoo.

PACIFIC BONITO AND SKIPJACK TUNA

Bonito and "skippies" are members of the mackerel/tuna family. They have a compact body just loaded for bear. Both are pelagic species and you're apt to find them cruising near the surface in open waters. Bonito and skipjack schools can build to impressive numbers. Their feeding habits are highly predictable. Identify where the bait populations roam and you've discovered "bonehead and skippie territory." Their diet is targeted toward fish and squid.

Consider these speedsters as both an inshore and offshore species. Their range is along the Pacific coastline of Baja and the lower Sea of Cortez. Peak months are July through September. The extended bite is from June through October. Boating is a necessity for locating and working schooling bonito and skipjack.

Caribbean Coast bonefish.

DORADO

At times they appear to outright fly. They can twist and gyrate like a whirling top. Then again, they can dive like a submarine. There's no telling what could happen once a dorado hits your streamer. One thing is certain, all mayhem breaks loose and it's a wild show to witness. Dorado have huge shoulders and a deeply compressed body. Their tail is forked, and you know that means they're a high speed predator.

They're an open ocean fish, yet dorado won't hesitate to cruise the inshore realm. Following bait, or any debris that could attract and hold bait populations, these hunters will travel anywhere it's necessary to feed. Fish, squid, and crustaceans are their diet.

Dorado are a wide ranging species in tropical and subtropical waters. Baja's Pacific coast, the Sea of Cortez, and Mexico's southern Pacific region are particularly strong for dorado populations. July, August, and September are peak months. May through November provides solid action in most locales.

ROOSTERFISH

This species has a family all its own. It does resemble a jack or pompano however. The body is deep and compressed. The tail is forked. The fin structure is short and stiff, with one notable exception. The rooster's leading dorsal fin is a series of seven exaggerated rays. This feature is often referred to as a "comb."

Though an inshore species, they feed heavily around the surf zone. Usually you can see them chasing baitfish along the outside breaks. It's also common to watch them enter the surfline to locate disoriented prey. It's a sure-fire thrill to see their "comb" break the surface while they're in hot pursuit of a meal.

Roosterfish are found along southern Baja, on both the Pacific and Cortez coasts. In Mexico they also range along the western mainland all the way down to Guatemala. Available year-round, the peak season is generally during summer. The extended bite lasts from May through November.

YELLOWTAIL

This game fish is a large powerful member of the amberjack family. Their range covers both inshore and offshore habitat. A free-roaming species, they prefer to be around rocky structures. Inshore you can also find them cruising the edges of kelp beds. The yellowtail feeds primarily on fish and squid populations. Crab and other pelagic crustaceans contribute to their diet as well.

Most common along the Baja's Pacific side, large populations of yellowtail can also be seen in the Sea of Cortez. Along northern Baja, the peak season occurs in the summer months. The extended bite lasts from April through October. Southern Baja's peak action takes place from April through June. The extended action can occur almost all year. Anglers working the north-central Sea of Cortez will find the best action during May, June, and July. The extended bite is from April to December.

YELLOWFIN TUNA

Solid muscle is their key to survival. This pelagic fish is often seen in massive schools. They search for fish and squid in the open ocean element. Once tuna locate their prey it can turn into an instant feeding frenzy. These fish can set the sea ablaze. It's an awesome sight if you've never experienced it. In fact, it's still an awesome sight even if you have experienced it before!

The yellowfin is found in most temperate and tropical seas. Major action occurs along the Baja. Both Pacific and Cortez coasts play host. Most of the action heats up from late spring through fall. July through September can bring peak action. The further south you travel, the longer the season lasts.

WAHOO

This fish also belongs to the mackerel family. They're a large, lean machine. Everything about their physique is adapted for high speed maneuvering. They don't often compose large schools, but seem to prefer hunting as semi-solitary predators. Wahoo generally hang around with marlin and other apex hunters of the open ocean.

The Sea of Cortez is where it's at for this marine rocket. Both the mainland and Baja coasts offer excellent action throughout the year. May through September will offer a good bite. November and December can bring peak action. Baja's Pacific side will also produce a strong bite. Look especially to the midsummer and early winter cycles.

STRIPED MARLIN

The billfish family has a grand compilation of sportfish in Mexican waters. The striped marlin is one of the most colorful and accessible members. This oceanic species truly prefers the offshore environment. The striped marlin is frequently encountered near the surface. Fish and squid are dominant in their diet. Like the smaller dorado, billfish will often be drawn to floating debris that could attract bait populations.

This spectacular game fish is caught throughout the eastern Pacific range. Major concentrations occur throughout the Sea of Cortez, as well as the Pacific side of Baja. Along Baja, August through October are good months. The north-central Cortez offers marlin from July through November. South, in the Cortez, peak months range from September through March.

Bill Sunderland with a prize Loreto yellowtail.

RICK E. MARTIN

Chapter FIVE

Tackle Tips

Stalking corbina in Northern Baja... but don't go barefoot!

Given the wide choice of today's market, many find the task of assembling their tackle to be a numbing experience. The fundamental process needn't be so. One of the more effective approaches is to systematically ask yourself what the key environmental factors will be, then fine-tune your selection by looking at the species you wish to target.

Once you've considered the basic environmental factors of wind direction and intensity, current speed, depth, structure, and cover, you're well on your way to narrowing the field of equipment suited for the job. If appropriate, add the possible influences of salt and ultraviolet invasion. The final adjustments to your tackle selection will be dictated by the behavior and anatomy of the game fish themselves. With this valuable information you'll soon be able to focus on the essentials necessary for your own Mexico adventure.

HABITAT NOTES AND QUICK REFERENCE GUIDE

Freshwater

The trout waters reconnoitered in Baja's northern mountains are basically small streams. You'll find yourself working in short- to medium-distance casting scenarios. The streambed is typical desert style habitat. You won't find much in the way of vegetative cover. There's plenty of casting room as the banks are wide-open terrain.

Bass reservoirs in Mexico are expansive bodies of water. Look for steep banks, chunk rock, tapering points, flats, floating cover (ie: hyacinth), and wood tangles. Most of your work will likely take place from a boat or float tube.

Rod and Reel Selections

Trout outfits will mirror your home waters. Three- through five-weight designs are outstanding choices.

Bass outfits of seven- through nine-weight designs are optimal. Rods with stout butt sections are preferred.

Line Options and Leader Systems

Trout lines should include a full floating design, and a sink-tip style as well. Your leader system will be based on two- to six-pound-test. Lengths will vary from 7 to 9 feet, with the rare occasion calling for extra tippet length.

Bass lines would include full floating, intermediate and fast sinking, or a set of shooting tapers. The terminal system is based on 8- to 12-pound-test. Lengths can vary from 5 to 9 feet. Knotless tapers are preferred for working around any heavy cover.

Sample Fly Patterns

Trout selection; Elk Hair Caddis, Hare's Ear Nymph, Humpy. Bass selection; Fire Bellied Newt, Hot Flash Minnow, Poppers, V-Worm.

The Tackle Bag

Hip boots are perfect for trout streams. Chest waders are really only necessary if you float-tube the bass waters.

Sample Species Include: Rainbow trout and largemouth bass.

SURF ZONE

The northern beaches can vary from small cobblestone (shingle-style beachhead) to finer grained sand. The farther you travel south in Mexico the more refined the sand particles become. The ultimate in sand quality is found along the Riviera and Caribbean coasts.

Troughs tend to be long down here. There's little in the way of holes, cuts, etc. Floating debris is minimal (except in a few places in the extreme northern sectors). Keep moving until you jump a school of game fish. Keep an eye peeled for any escaping baitfish activity.

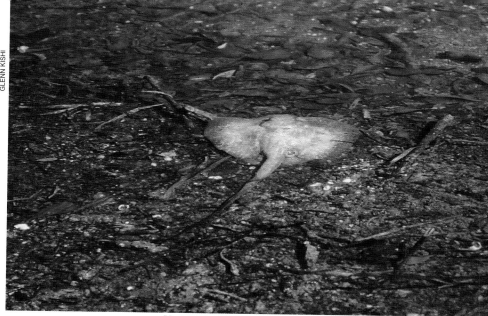

You need proper protection any time you wade in Mexico.

Rod and Reel Selections

Seven- through nine-weight outfits are perfect. Keep in mind that you need to handle the heavy hydraulics as well as the game fish. Saltwater designs are essential for both rod and reel. This is a nasty habitat with potential for grinding sand-n-salt into your tackle.

Line Options and Leader Systems

Shooting tapers are a real plus working in this environment. Using modified designs, like the Teeny Saltwater Series, are also terrific. Fast-sinking lines will be your cornerstone choices. There's not much call for a floating style line out here.

Leader systems can be kept fairly short. Most situations call for around 6 feet in length. Your tippet should test around 8- to 12-pound depending on the quarry you wish to target. You might want to add a short bite trace (30-pound) if you plan on chasing flatfish.

Sample Fly Patterns

Grass Shrimp, Lefty's Deceivers, Popovics' Surf Candy, Rabbitron Crab, Surf Grub.

The Tackle Bag

Never wade in the surf zone barefoot. I prefer to use neoprene boots for safety (against rays, jellyfish, etc.). I also prefer to use ultra-light waders in northern waters (I can roll the top down if necessary). Considering a stripping basket? They aren't required, but it's a nice addition for line control in the Mexican surf.

Sample Species Include: Surfperch, corbina, corvina, flatfish, ladyfish, and jacks.

FLATS AND ESTUARY

Expect to deal with heavy wind activity on the flats. You'll find the habitat and game fish require you to make numerous medium- to long-range casts. Moving targets are the name of the game. You can either wade the flats or work from a casting platform on a skiff.

The mangrove estuary is more of a short- to medium-range game. You'll be working tight to thick cover and structure. Your casts will often be made to specific ambush stations for apex predators. Estuary environs will also present you with shifting sandbars, at times reorienting channels and holes. Baitfish and game fish alike

Spectra-type lines will add capacity and strength to your system.

will travel along the main currents of this unsettled habitat. Most of your work will take place from a boat.

Rod and Reel Selections

Flats anglers generally prefer to work with seven- or eight-weight outfits for bonefish. Your reel design should have one of the finest drag systems available. Many anglers are showing a preference for "rapid retrieve" (large arbor) style reels. The spool should be capable of carrying a minimum of 100 yards of 20-pound backing.

If you wish to tackle larger game (permit, tarpon, etc.) consider using a nine-weight outfit. You can go heavier if you wish, but it's not usually necessary for Mexico's flats and estuary game. You do however need to upgrade your reel selection so the spool capacity will handle 200 yards of backing or more.

Mangrove estuaries can be tough and testy—a nine-weight outfit can give you an edge for handling large game in tight quarters. Again, if you feel more confident with a heavier outfit by all means use it.

Both flats and estuary scenarios are typically served with a rod blank that favors a quick tip design. Your choice in rods should allow you to work in a rapid fashion, at any casting distance.

Again, a rod blank with a stout butt section can be an advantage in both of these arenas as well. You'll need the ability to immediately move a game fish from tangles or redirect it from heading out to open sea.

Line Options and Leader Systems

Floating designs are the cornerstone to flats fishing. Since you're working with high heat, extreme sun, saltwater, and possibly strong winds, a line made to address the impacts of these conditions is essential. Full floating "saltwater tapers" can make a difference in your field performance. Consider a slow-sinking version to add versatility to your outfit.

Your terminal selection is based on a tapered 9-foot length. It's common to extend this system with extra tippet material rated from 6- to 12-pound-test. You'll need material that can handle the abrasive effects of coral and various reef cover.

The unique anatomy of a tarpon or barracuda's mouth demands specific adjustments in your terminal tackle. Barracuda, for example, need a wire bite trace. I recommend you purchase pre-tied systems for both of these game fish.

Mangrove situations often dictate sinking style lines. Slow- to medium-sink rates are best. Shooting tapers are ideal for working in this kind of habitat. Floating lines will have plenty of opportunities as well in the estuary realm. Their application excels in shallow waters (particularly presenting flies to snook). Weight-forward tapers are an outstanding choice with floating line designs.

Terminal tackle for working the mangroves is based on 5- to 7-foot leaders. You can extend the system as needed. Generally tippets rated for the 10- to 16-pound range will be fine. Casting to snook or tarpon will require a shock trace (adding heavier abrasion resistant mono rated from 30 to 60 pounds).

Sample Fly Patterns

Apte Too Plus (Black Death), Barracuda Fly, Blanton's Sar-Mul-Mac, Chico Bonefish Special, Cockroach, Crazy Charlies, Dahlberg Saltwater Diver, Del's Permit Crab, Grass Shrimp, Gurgler Fly, Mini Puffs, Rabbitron Crab, Red & White Tarpon, Surf Grub.

It takes more than one line to tackle Mexico's game fish.

The Tackle Bag

Polarized glasses are a must. You can't live without them on the flats. I believe footwear is critical for safety as you wade.

Sample Species Include: Bonefish, permit, tarpon, barracuda, and snook.

ROCKY SHORE AND KELP BEDS

Anglers afoot or afloat can enjoy the rocky shore experience. From gentle sloping tidal shelves to steep, plummeting cliffs, the variety of structure and cover here is incredible. The "rocky experience" isn't limited to the mainland as you'll find it also exists around islands, offshore reefs, and sea pinnacles.

Kelp beds can be a part of the rocky shore environment. More often you'll find the beds have anchored themselves outside the casting range of foot anglers. Small skiffs or pangas are the best way to explore these marine forests.

Cutlery is an integral part of your tackle selection.

Wave surge and complex currents are key in the formation of shoreline habitat. The environment is frequently abrasive and cluttered with snags. You can't be shy about working your tackle here. As the saying goes "no guts, no glory." Kelp offers you the option of working along edges and pockets. If you get caught day dreamin' you could get trapped-n-wrapped out here as well!

Rod and Reel Selections

Considering the complexities of this realm, nine- to eleven-weight outfits are terrific choices. I find the nine-weight is fine for working in fairly open waters. The heavier outfits are a clear advantage in tight structure and cover.

Reels and rods should be of saltwater design. You need the

capability of working with heavy terminal tackle, larger knots and flies, and strong game fish.

Line Options and Leader Systems

Basically sinking lines are the top producers around rock and kelp environs. Shooting tapers are a very effective system here. Heads rated for fast-sinking applications are the foundation choice. In addition, slower-sinking and Deep-Water Express models will expand your outfit's capabilities.

The leader system is pretty simple. Keep it short and stout. The basic length is around 6 feet overall. You can work with tippets rated from 10- to 16-pound-test. You might wish to add a shock trace (30- to 60-pound) depending on the game fish you pursue. Generally you won't need a shock trace for any of the bass-like species.

Sample Fly Patterns

Blanton's Sea Arrow Squid, Blanton's Tropical Punch, Crystal Popper, Lefty's Deceivers, V-Worm.

The Tackle Bag

Be prepared to change leaders or tippets as they can weaken from abuse. Pre-tied systems using a loop-to-loop connection are great. Keep your hooks sharpened (a flat bastard file works wonders).

Sample Species Include: Calico bass, sand bass, various pargo and cabrilla.

INSHORE

Everyone has a slightly different image of what the "inshore" habitat might be. For the purposes of this book, I'm referring to the waters occurring just outside the breakers, and always having a shoreline in view (even if the latter represents 10 miles out to sea). Generally the game fish here are available much closer than you'd expect.

You'll find the depths out here can vary dramatically. The currents will shift with the seasons. Sometimes there's floating cover, other days a barren ocean surface. Shoreline structure and bottom cover are still factors in many game fish's behavior.

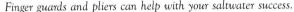
Finger guards and pliers can help with your saltwater success.

GLENN KISHI

GLENN KISHI

Knots and rigging skills can make the difference.

Rod and Reel Selections

The majority of your work will take place with 10- to 12-weight outfits. You need to have confidence when you tackle these game fish. Medium- to long-range casts will dominate the game.

Reels must have outstanding drag systems, large-line capabilities, and carry plenty of line capacity. The use of Spectra-type backing will increase the reel's performance. Large arbor designs are favored by many inshore anglers. Anti-reverse reels are another option used by many.

Line Options and Leader Systems

Sinking style lines are most often called for. Shooting tapers will offer you a great deal of versatility. Carry heads ranging from slow-sinking to Deep-Water Express models. Saltwater floating tapers can be used for popper and shallow streamer presentations to complete your collection of lines.

Your terminal system is typically short (around 5 feet). An example would include using a few feet of 50-pound-test mono for the butt section, adding about 15 to 20 inches of class tippet, and then finishing with a foot of shock trace. Of course, you could always just use a straight three-foot section of mono off your butt section if you prefer. Try to avoid long leaders that are subject to abrading.

Sample Fly Patterns

Baja Streaker, Balsa Poppers, Beadle Blue Water Deceivers, Blanton's Sar-Mul-Mac, Blanton's Sea Arrow Squid, Blanton's Tropical Punch, Combs' Sea Habit Bucktails, Crystal Poppers, Curcione Tuna Tonic, Dahlberg Saltwater Diver, Lefty's Deceivers.

The Tackle Bag

I believe the following items go beyond the term "accessory."

1. You can't beat a first-class knife. Single fixed-blade styles are real workhorses. If you use a collapsible design, try to work with a model that locks the blade when it's in an open position.
2. Have a top-notch quality pair of pliers. They can assist you with knot assembly, cutting heavy mono or light wire, hook removal, etc.
3. A multi-use tool such as a Leatherman can be invaluable.

You need extra protection against abrasive bills and such.

RAY BEADLE

4. The use of finger socks, an archer's glove, or similar hand protection is a real asset.

Sample Species Include: Dorado, roosterfish, yellowtail, bonito, and sierra.

OFFSHORE

Well here we are in the arena of the heavyweights. It's all about big water, big game, big tackle, and hopefully big fun! This is the habitat of true pelagic species, creatures who rely heavily on oceanic currents and following the nuances of temperature shifts in the sea. It's rare to find these game fish close to shore. Billfish and other apex predators are highly conditioned for their endurance travel. This "on the go" lifestyle requires massive amounts of food to sustain each game fish.

Rod and Reel Selections

There's no room for error in this league of fly fishing. Equipment demands will be extreme. You need everything an inshore outfit offers you, only this class will be upgraded to handle 12- to 15-weight designs. The rod needs to have lifting power. The reel needs the best drag system and generous line capacity. Anti-reverse reels are used by many blue-water anglers.

Line Options and Leader Systems

Line designs basically mirror the inshore game, only upgraded to fit the appropriate rod and reel combination with which you're working. Most systems are designed around shooting heads and modified lines. Your collection of lines should include a slow-sinking salt-water taper, medium-sinking billfish taper, and a Deep-Water Express or lead-core head.

The following system is recommended by many of the top rods in the blue-water game: start with 20- or 30-pound Dacron backing, splice on 30- or 50-pound Spectra style running line, add 60 feet of running line from an eight-weight sinking bonefish taper, add your shooting head and complete the system with your terminal rigging. Incorporating the Spectra running line will provide you with a staggering amount of working material (depending on your reel it could equal 600 yards or better!)

Terminal rigging can make or break your success out here. The use of Bimini knots and other specialty connections are directed for high impact, high abrasion, and long bouts with the toughest of game fish. All-purpose leaders are often 8 feet or longer. One popular formula consists of 60% butt section, 20% taper, and 20% tippet material. Billfish leaders are typically 5 feet or less. A common system would include a few feet of butt section, 16 to 18 inches of class tippet, and a foot of shock trace. I suggest you consult with your fly shop or guide service to get specific information in constructing these offshore rigs.

Sample Fly Patterns

Baird Squid Fly, Baja Streaker, Beadle Blue Water Deceivers, Blanton's Sar-Mul-Mac, Blanton's Sea Arrow Squid, Combs' Green Machine, Combs' Sea Habit Billfish, Combs' Sea Habit Deceivers, Howe's ALF series, Kanz Mylar Minnow, Lefty's Deceivers.

The Tackle Bag

Again, you should have first-rate tools capable of handling the tasks of heavy rigging. Stretchers are a great addition for storing pre-rigged flies on heavy leaders. From knives and pliers, to hook files and spare reel parts, you can't have enough insurance in your tackle bag. Offshore adventures require you to be prepared for everything!

You'll probably need full hand-protection. Popular glove styles include batting, golf, and cycling gloves.

Many of the offshore experts recommend using fighting belts for additional power and support.

Sample Species Include: Marlin, sailfish, tuna, and wahoo.

SOME THOUGHTS ON RIGGING

One of the most overlooked aspects of tackle selection and field technique is the use of appropriate knots in your system. I can't place enough emphasis on how important this skill is to your success. As fly fishers, we can't control the water conditions, or the weather patterns for that matter. When it comes right down to it, there are just a few things we do have dominion over. Knot selection and tying execution is clearly an aspect of the sport where we have complete control.

Taking the extra time to properly construct your terminal system can be the difference between a triumphant portrait or maddening knot failure. If you think about it, there really isn't any excuse for knot failure. There's an abundance of specialty knots for just about any fishing application you can think of. Balancing your rigging to match both species and habitat is just as critical as choosing the right pattern to match a hatch or represent a member of schooling baitfish.

Here are five knots that will help you increase your chance for success in Mexico. The tying instructions for the following knots can be found in *Practical Fishing Knots #2* (Lefty Kreh and Mark Sosin), and *Bluewater Fly Fishing* (by Trey Combs).

Albright Special

This is a utility tie you can use at various junctures in your system. It works wonders for connecting lines that have dissimilar diameters. It also excels when used for pairing lines made from different materials. The Albright's breaking strength is around 95%.

Bimini Twist

Universally, this is the knot recognized for tough saltwater use. Ask anyone that works the seas for a living—"you gotta know it and use it." The Bimini's breaking strength is rated at 100%.

Lefty's Non-Slip Loop

Lefty Kreh designed this simple knot, which works particularly well connecting your fly to very large diameter/heavy materials. The loop's breaking strength is rated at 100%.

Five-Turn Surgeon's Loop

This is a quick knot to assemble and it gives your fly great action. Use the knot for a pre-rigged fly and tippet combo. This loop design was developed by Florida tarpon guide Steve Huff. The Five-Turn's breaking strength is rated at 100%.

Palomar Knot

Here's one of my favorite connections to the fly. The extra mono around the eye is like an insurance package against the effects of abrasion. The Palomar's breaking strength is 100%.

One final note concerning rigging: Saltwater experts highly recommend the use of Pliobond and other appropriate adhesives to coat your knots for extra security.

Destinations Introduction

The following chapters outline specific information from the five major regions around the country. Hub cities, lodging and camping, transportation access, and of course, fly fishing related data is presented. Every precaution has been taken to accurately portray the region and services available. It is inevitable that change will occur. Use the information presented in this guide as a launch point to begin your journey down south. It would be prudent to check with a travel agent for current transportation and lodging options if appropriate. If you choose to explore the lesser-known, and more remote locations, stay flexible and keep a sense of humor. Your excursion through Mexico's great countryside is worth all the twists of fate!

The following outline format is presented for each of the five regions.

1. A general description of the countryside.
2. Each target city (and environs) will feature the following;
    a. Fly Fishing Options
    b. Highlight Species
    c. Area Access (includes air travel, cruise lines, and land vehicles as appropriate.)
    d. Lodging, Camping/RV Options
    e. Charters/Guide Services

Chapter SIX

Northwest Coast and Mainland

It was just days before Thanksgiving and I had plenty on my mind. It had nothing to do with the holiday, in fact that was the furthest thing from my thoughts. All I could focus on was how hard that bass just exploded on the fly. It wasn't even sunrise yet and Andy Burk and I were getting pulverized by pugnacious largemouths. Huge rafts of hyacinth presented the perfect ambush canopy from which the fish would demolish our poppers. The action was absolutely fierce. And standing next to Burk during that kind of bedlam bordered on the insane. We were two casting machines in motion—with only one functional brain between us! The laughter alone was enough to rock any boat.

It was the first day of four bass-filled adventures on Lake El Salto. In reality it was the first 30 minutes on the water, and we proceeded to make every presentation error you could imagine. We had "bass fever" and couldn't shake it worth a darn. Poppers smacked against the boat, impossible tangles grew from misplaced shots, even knots failed us. Yup, there we were, two bassin' assassins getting pummeled with humility.

Things finally ground to a complete halt. We sat in the middle of the boat looking like two hysterical heaps. Each one silently grateful

Working the fenceline at sunrise on Lake Dominquez.

Rafts of hyacinth play a major role in bass cover.

that the other didn't record any blackmail shots, I'm sure. Taking a few moments to reconstruct our tackle, we regrouped and made our first quality casts into the waning darkness. S-M-A-S-H . . . FISH ON!!! It was an auspicious way to hail the day.

Our neighbors to the south have a treasure chest for freshwater adventure. Bass are to Mexico, what salmon are to Alaska; they're bountiful, they're big, and they're accessible. Mexico is becoming a Mecca for world-class largemouth bass. Pioneering spirits like Billy Chapman Jr. and Roberto Balderrama have created a phenomenal resource among the reservoirs and rivers of the northwestern region. For nearly four decades they've managed properties to produce healthy, viable trophy populations.

In November 1994, the Mexican government granted game fish status to largemouth bass, taking the first step in addressing commercial-netting limits and other threats to the future of the fishery. Netting has been banned on a few of the reservoirs, but catch-and-release fishing is practiced by only a few lodges and tourist camps. If catch-and-release is to become commonplace, the region's farmers and fishermen need an assured income from the sport angling community. I'm sure the future will be bright because the fly fishing industry for largemouth continues to expand.

The saltwater scene is no less prolific. Sport angling has a well established industry around the Sea of Cortez. From marlin to corvina it's your choice and the entire region can accommodate your desires. The northwest area encompasses the states of Sonora and Sinaloa. Their coastline offers you a wealth of small bays and braided mangrove estuaries for exploration. The coastal region also affords easy access to rugged islands offshore and blue-water habitat.

High desert plateau is the paramount feature of the Sonoran district's interior. Cactus-studded open space is characteristic of the wild and primitive landscape. The southern sector of the state is influenced by the mountainous Sierra Madre Occidental range. Sonora's sinuous rivers have been tamed to create massive reservoirs in the higher elevations.

Continuing south into Sinaloa, the Sierra Madre provides a lush scene. Palm trees, even pine stands, cover the mountain's deep green valleys. The powerful Rio Fuerte, and the Rio Sinaloa, are the source of refreshment for much of the state. The reservoirs of the Sierra foothills are a direct response to the growing development of this region. As a farming district, Sinaloa's lowlands are vibrant with produce.

Access to the northwest region is a breeze. Six airports service the area. A major highway system travels the entire coastline. Extensive surface streets and unimproved roads weave themselves through city and backcountry alike. Hub cities of the northwest will include Puerto Penasco, Hermosillo, Guaymas, Los Mochis, Culiacán, and Mazatlán.

Those of you driving can access the area by using Mexico Highway 2 or Mexico Highway 15. Both have entry points along the Arizona border. Each of the highways has been renovated and are much improved. Toll payments are required to travel the new highways. The free routes are slower, and are in inferior condition.

Travel by air is supported by the following carriers: Aeromexico, Mexicana Airlines, and Aero California. Mazatlán is also serviced by Delta Airlines, and Alaska Airlines.

Even though we'll outline the hub city options for you, the coastal areas between these cities can provide spectacular fishing. The farther you move away from a hub city, the more remote the coastline becomes. It can be completely inaccessible by land vehicle in expansive stretches.

PUERTO PENASCO (ROCKY POINT)
Fly Fishing Options
Strong for inshore, rocky shore, and surf zone opportunities. The beaches and surf are outstanding around this part of the northwest coast. There are also major structures to explore in Bahia de Adair, and in the nearby Bahia San Jorge. Try working around Pinto and Pelican points for reef action. The patches of volcanic shoreline are quite impressive around Puerto Penasco. Be aware that extreme swings in the tide will occur in this area.

Commercial shrimp boats work extensively in The Cortez.

Highlight Species
Corvina, pompano, pargo, dorado, yellowtail, sierra, mackerel, jacks, halibut, opaleye, ladyfish, croaker.

Area Access
The town of Puerto Penasco is located approximately 65 miles across the border. Most drivers enter at the Sonoita crossing (near Lukeville, Arizona) and proceed along Mexico Highway 8.

Lodging, Camping/RV Options
Costa Brava, Hotel Playa Hermosa, Motel Senorial, Playa Bonita

Hotel, Motel Mar y Sol, Hotel Viña del Mar. Camping is best done a few miles from town at Sandy Beach. RV parks include Clomar Trailer Park, Playa Bonito, Playa Miramar, and Playa de Oro.

Charters/Guide Service
Charters are available near Pelican Point (El Faro Sociedad Cooperativa de Produccion Turista). Pangas can be hired around the Bahia de la Choya boating facilities.

HERMOSILLO

Fly Fishing Options
Located inland, this area has great largemouth action at Lake Novillo (approx. 50 miles east to Mazatlán, another 38 to the dam). The lake can be hard to find. Saltwater adventures abound around Bahia Kino, west of Hermosillo (approx. 65 miles). Inshore, rocky shore, and surf-zone opportunities exist.

Highlight Species
Largemouth bass, yellowtail, dorado, tuna, pargo, sierra, sand bass, corvina, jacks, croaker, ladyfish, triggerfish.

Area Access
Hermosillo is located right on Mexico Highway 15. Lake Novillo is on a secondary roadway. Bahia Kino is at the end of Mexico Highway 16 (well paved). You can fly into Hermosillo on Aeromexico and Mexicana.

Lodging, Camping/RV Options
Hotel San Alberto, Hotel Monte Carlo, Hotel Posada de Mar, and Holiday Inn Hermosillo. Lodging in Bahia Kino includes Posada del Mar, Santa Gemma Hotel. RV parks include Kino Bay Motel/RV, Caverna del Seri Trailor Park, and Islandia Marina Trailer Park. Camping can be outstanding for do-it-yourselfers.

Charters/Guide Service
There are no charters available in Bahia Kino, however, you can rent pangas on the beach in Old Kino.

GUYAMAS

Fly Fishing Options
Outstanding big-game prospects because of the "Guyamas Trench." Offshore, inshore, rocky shore, and surf zone action is available. There are many islands to explore as well. Guyamas has two bays; Bahia de San Carlos (great surf-zone action) and Bahia Bacochibampo (excellent offshore/inshore access). East of Guyamas lies solid largemouth bass fishing at Lake Obregon.

Highlight Species
Marlin, dorado, yellowtail, wahoo, tuna, pargo, cabrilla, corvina, sierra, jacks, croaker, triggerfish, sand bass, largemouth bass.

Area Access
This is now a major port and resort area. It's located about 85 miles south of Hermosillo. Just continue on Mexico Highway 15 straight into town. You can fly into Guyamas with Aeromexico. To reach Lake Obregon you must drive south on Mexico Highway 15 until the town of Esperanza. From there the dam is approximately 30 miles east.

Lodging, Camping/RV
Del Puerto Motel, Motel Flamingos, Malibu Motel, Hotel Playa de Cortez, Leo's Inn, and Hotel Armida. Camping is not permitted on the beaches in town. Drive south of town to find solitude for pitching a tent. Lodging at Bahia San Carlos includes Hotel Fiesta San Carlos, Motel Creston, and Solimar Hotel and Country Club. RV parks include the facility at Shangi-La Trailer Park, Totonaka Trailer Park, and Hacienda Tetakawi Trailer Park.

Charters/Guide Service
You can rent pangas and charter cruisers from Guyamas Marina on Bacochibampo Bay.

LOS MOCHIS

Fly Fishing Options
There's outstanding largemouth action in the reservoirs of the Sierra Madre foothills (Huite, Baccarac, Hidalgo, and Dominquez lakes). Saltwater action consists of offshore, inshore, rocky shore, estuary, and surf-zone possibilities. Extensive mangrove estuaries exist both north and south of Bahia Ohuira. Roca El Farallon offers great off-shore island habitat.

Highlight Species
Snook, yellowtail, roosterfish, tuna, marlin, wahoo, pargo, cabrilla, jacks, triggerfish, barracuda, sand bass, sierra, croaker, largemouth bass.

Vast estuaries offer you solitude and great game fish.

Area Access

Mexico Highway 15 is the main artery. A secondary road takes you west to the village of Topolobampo and Bahia Ohuira. Unimproved access can take you north of town to Nueva Pascola and Ahome (to explore the massive mangrove system). Air travelers can fly into Los Mochis via Aeromexico and Aero California. Access to the largemouth reservoirs are east of the city on highway 32, or south of Los Mochis out of Guasave.

Lodging, Camping/RV

Hotel Beltran, Hotel America, and Plaza Inn Motel. RV parks include Hotel Colinas RV Park and Los Mochis Copper Canyon RV Park. Camping is great on the island Santa María (located in Bahia Ohuira).

Charters/Guide Service

Pangas are available on the beach at Topolobampo. Charters can be hired at the Club de Nautico.

CULIACAN

Fly Fishing Options

Located a bit inland, this is a fine place for largemouth expeditions (Mateos and Sanalona lakes). Saltwater options include inshore, rocky shore, estuary and surf zone. The area around Isla Tachita and Isla Altamura is well worth the effort (near Altata). Isla Santa María is another spot worth exploring (near El Dorado).

Highlight Species

Marlin, tuna, wahoo, pargo, cabrilla, sierra, jacks, corvina, barracuda, yellowtail, dorado, sand bass, largemouth bass.

Area Access

Mexico Highway 15. The bass locales are on secondary roadways east of town. Coastal access is on Highway 30 and other secondary routes. Aero California and Aeromexico service the area.

Lodging, Camping/RV

Hotel San Marcos, Hotel San Francisco, Hotel El Mayo, Hotel San Luis Lindavista. RV parking is available at Motel Tres Rios. The coastal region is pretty remote, camping can take place most anywhere.

Charters/Guide Service

Pangas can be hired in the villages of Altata and El Dorado.

MAZATLÁN

Fly Fishing Options

Outstanding big game and inshore prospects. Estuary and surf-zone habitat abound. Largemouth bass are world-class at Lake El Salto.

Highlight Species

Marlin, wahoo, tuna, yellowtail, dorado, sierra, snook, pargo, corvina, cabrilla, barracuda, roosterfish, sand bass, largemouth bass.

Area Access

Mexico Highway 15 takes you right to the heart of town. The airport is serviced by Aeromexico, Mexicana, Aero California, Delta, and Alaska airlines. El Salto is accessed east along Highway 40.

Lodging, Camping/RV

Hotel La Siesta, Hotel Aquamarina, Hotel Sands, Hotel Playa Mazatlán, Hotel Beltran, El Cid Resort. Camping is very popular in the area. RV parks include Bungalow/Trailer Park Playa Escondida, La Posta Trailer Park, and Mar Rosa Park.

Charters/Guide Services

There are numerous charters available at the marinas in town. Pangas can be hired in Mazatlán's marinas and the surrounding villages.

TEACAPAN

Fly Fishing Options

Immense mangrove estuary system and surf-zone habitat. The inland system includes Estero Teacapan, Estero Aqua Grande (with Isla La Palma), and Laguna Aqua Grande. The entire waterway offers over 30 miles of exploration. The massive Laguna Aqua Brava system links itself to the south via Estero Puerto del Rio.

The beaches are wide open with mile after mile of surf rolling in. Boaters might wish to work the area around Isla del Otro Lado outside the mouth of the Estero Teacapan.

Highlight Species

Snook, sierra, pargo, corvina, croaker, jacks.

Area Access

Approximately 65 miles south of Mazatlan. Drive Mexico Highway 15 south to the junction of Escuinapa del Hidalgo. Turn onto the narrow paved road to Teacapan (southwest approximately 25 miles).

Lodging, Camping/RV

Lupita's Resort and Motor Park, Hotel Denisse.

Charters/Guide Services

No charters available. Pangas can be rented along the beach.

ADVENTURES BEYOND IMAGES

A massive estuary exists around Teacapan.

Chapter SEVEN

The Riviera and Southwest Coast

Pangas are the "taxi of the seas."

Initially, the state of Oaxaca caught my interest due to its vast wilderness and mountainous terrain. The high country of the Sierra Madre del Sur provided the backdrop for visions anew. It represented a land of unclimbed routes, a land of unknown challenges. Oaxaca's extensive wilderness also represented wild river flows and treasures hidden in remote jungles. The adventurer in me rejoiced for such a prime location to exercise the skills I'd acquired after years of expedition work.

Expanding my explorations southward brought me to the breathtaking coastal range of the Sierra de Miahuatlan. The impressive sculpted coastline rekindled my adventurous passion, only this time with a different emphasis. I was determined to return with a fly rod to discover the hidden treasures in the Gulf of Tehuantepec.

I poured over journals and searched for accounts of fly fishing excursions in the southwest's waters. If fly fishing pioneers had indeed discovered these bays I couldn't find any evidence. It was clearly a circumstance that required a first-hand exploration. It was just the kind of challenge I relish, with the magic I value the most. The waters are nothing short of intoxicating; a dreamscape for fly-rodding adventure.

Mexico's Riviera and southwestern communities share a continuous coastline that spans nearly 1,800 miles. At the northernmost point lies the Tropic of Cancer. The southern border is shared with Guatemala.

The Riviera is legendary. Its mega-resorts have molded the district's lifestyle into one of intense recreational pursuits. The area's sportsfishing ranks as some of the best in the world. You'll find a well-developed fleet of blue-water cruisers prepared to take you to their fruitful offshore arena.

If the resort scene isn't your style, don't fret, the new coastal road system affords access to numerous outlying villages and remote beaches. Locations outside of the mega-resorts rarely get much pressure from tourists. Don't let the term "new coastal road system" bring images of exclusively high-tech highways. I am referring to the total system, including unimproved roads providing direct oceanside access.

The hub cities found along Mexico's Riviera Coast consist of Puerto Vallarta, Manzanillo, Ixtapa-Zihuatanejo, and Acapulco. The following air carriers provide service to the region; Aeromexico, Aero California, Mexicana, Delta, American, Alaska, and Continental airlines.

The Southwest Coast is without a doubt the least traveled sector on Mexico's Pacific side. In fact, it just might be the least frequented in all of Mexico. This 900-mile coast offers dramatic seascapes and a lush mountainous interior. The coastal environs are dominated by tiny coves and remote beachheads. The idyllic waters glisten like diamonds. This region is perfect for the truly adventurous at heart.

Mexico's government has targeted the state of Oaxaca for development as a major tourist destination. You'll find the changing face, and pace, of the small fishing villages showing signs of the 20-

plus-year plan. Regardless of the development, I feel the sector is a must see for anyone looking to explore a ripe new fly-fishing territory.

Along the Southwest Coast, hub sites include Puerto Escondido, Huatulco, and Salina Cruz. Flying into these locales you'll find service provided by Aeromexico, Aerovias Oaxaquenas, and Mexicana airlines.

Those of you driving through the Riviera and southwestern countryside will find Mexico Highway 200 the main artery. The highway hugs the coastline and presents you with the most extensive options for touring the entire area. "200" can be a pretty rough ride through certain stretches. It would behoove you to program extra time to negotiate the roads down there. Recently the government has made a commitment to upgrade the region as a prime tourist destination. Some of those finances and resources might actually find their way toward repairing the road system. The task would be immense as the coastal area alone is over 1,800 miles long.

If you fly into Mexico City and choose to rent a vehicle, Mexico Highway 95 will take you directly to Acapulco. Another option out of the capitol is Mexico Highway 190. This route will take you past the mountainous locale of Oaxaca City, and on toward the settlements of Tehuantepec and the Salina Cruz coastal environs.

Cruise ships are another option for travel to this part of Mexico. The Riviera is a world-class destination for super luxury liners. The major ports of Mazatlán, Puerto Vallarta, and Acapulco provide year-round service. The international carriers include Carnival, Princess, and Royal Caribbean.

A surf-caught jack near Topolobampo.

PUERTO VALLARTA

Fly Fishing Options

"PV" is a renowned area for big-game opportunities. Both inshore and offshore options abound. Take the time to work around Islas Marietas and Los Arcos.

Highlight Species

Marlin, sailfish, roosterfish, dorado, wahoo, yellowtail, tuna, bonito, pargo, cabrilla, jacks, sierra.

Area Access

Traveling from Mazatlán to the north, Mexico Highway 15 intersects Highway 200 at the city of Tepic. Use 200 for direct access south into Puerto Vallarta. "PV" is about 100 miles south of Tepic. Those of you flying will utilize Puerto Vallarta's Gustavo Diaz Ordaz International Airport. The site is serviced by Mexicana, Alaska, Delta, Aeromexico, American, Continental, and Aero California airlines. Cruise ships using this port-of-call include Royal Caribbean, Holland-America, Norwegian, Princess, and Carnival cruise lines.

Lodging, Camping/RV Options

Facilities run the full range. Try the following suggestions; Fiesta Americana, Hacienda Buenaventura, Playa Los Arcos, Posada de Roger, Hotel Yasmin, Hotel Marlyn, Hotel Oro Verde. Camping isn't allowed on most of the beaches near town. A great location is on the Playa Las Animas (boating offers the only access). RV and tent options also include the Puerto Vallarta Trailer Park and Tacho's Trailer Park.

Mike Wolverton working a rocketing marlin.

RAY BEADLE

Charters/Guide Service

Hotels can arrange for full charters and rentals. Services are also available along the waterfront and the marina. Pangas can be rented at Playa de Oro, Playa Mismaloya, and Boca de Tomatlán.

CHAMELA AND BARRA DE NAVIDAD

Fly Fishing Options

Inshore, offshore, rocky shore, and surf-zone potential are rich around this region. The beaches are generally wild and uncrowded. Rocky points and coves offer plenty of structure and terrific small-craft opportunities.

Highlight Species

Marlin, roosterfish, dorado, yellowtail, tuna, wahoo, bonito, mackerel, pargo, cabrilla, sierra, jacks.

Area Access

You can fly into Playa de Oro International Airport near Manzanillo, or the Puerto Vallarta airport. If you are traveling by land, the "Chamela/Barra" area is located off Mexico Highway 200. I'd like to point out that the road conditions can vary widely depending on the weather around here (particularly during the rainy season). To gain direct access to the Barra de Navidad coast you'll be required to use a secondary road.

Rocky shore habitat can be found almost anywhere in Mexico.

Lodging, Camping/RV Options

Both the El Tecuan and Coco's Hotel Melaque offer great services around the Chamela stretch of coast-line. In Barra de Navidad is the Hotel Delfin and the Cabo Blanco. Camping is fine along most of the beaches; outstanding opportunities can be found on Playa Tenacatita and Boca de Iguanas. RV options near Chamela are best at Villa Polinesia. Near Barra de Navidad try the site offered at Boca de Iguana.

Charters/Guide Service

Hotels can arrange for full services and rentals. Pangas are available at Playa Tenacatita, Playa Los Angeles Locos, Boca de Iguana, and the lagoon in Barra.

MANZANILLO

Fly Fishing Options

Two adjoining bays showcase the waters down here. Bahia Manzanillo and Bahia Santiago provide a spectacular setting for sportsfishing. An abundance of rocky habitat and wide-open beaches are prime locations to cast your fly. Inshore, offshore, rocky shore, and surf-zone opportunities are for the taking.

Highlight Species

Sailfish, marlin, wahoo, dorado, yellowtail, tuna, bonito, mackerel, pargo, cabrilla, jacks, sierra.

Area Access

Drivers take note: the stretch of 200 leading into the Manzanillo area is less than ideal. Caution is the key to driving around this area. The Playa de Oro Airport handles Aeromexico and Mexicana airlines.

Lodging, Camping/RV Options

Try the following choices: Parador Marbella, Hotel Colonial, La Posada, Hotel Star, Fiesta Mexicana, Condotel Arco Iris, and Sierra Radisson Plaza. RV opportunities exist at the El Palmar Trailer Park.

Charters/Guide Service

Hotels can arrange for full services and rentals. Pangas are available at Playa Miramar and Playa La Audiencia. The government has announced a significant commitment to design a new marina and accompanying resort for the area.

IXTAPA-ZIHUATANEJO

Fly Fishing Options

Big-game action soars in this region. Offshore, inshore, rocky shore, and surf-zone habitats are available to explore. The area is relatively new compared to Mazatlán and other mega sites. Only recently has the sportsfishing community begun to expand here. Their efforts have been rewarded with a solid year-round fishery. World-class catches in uncrowded waters await anglers venturing into this fertile domain.

Highlight Species

Sailfish, roosterfish, marlin, wahoo, dorado, yellowtail, tuna, bonito, mackerel, pargo, cabrilla, jacks, sierra.

Schoolie dorado lit up like a neon sign.

Ray Beadle's Blue Water Deceiver for wahoo.

Perfect seas can be found along the Southwest Coast.

Area Access
Mexico Highway 200 takes you into the area. Secondary roads will provide direct access to the waterfront. If you fly in, the Ixtapa-Zihuatanejo International Airport is serviced by Mexicana, Aeromexico, and Delta.

Lodging, Camping/RV Options
The area offers a wide spectrum of facilities including a Club Med. Westin Camino Real, Hotel Tres Marías, La Casita, Hotel Avila, and Villas Miramar are all fine choices. Los Buzos Trailer Park offers RV support. Camping on Isla Ixtapa is great around Playa Carey.

Charters/Guide Service
Hotels will be happy to arrange for full services and rentals. Pangas are available at the marina and along the waterfront.

ACAPULCO

Fly Fishing Options
Don't let the mega resort atmosphere scare you, the place can produce some wonderful fly-rod action. Offshore, inshore, and rocky shore habitat can be explored. Surf-zone options are limited somewhat by crowded beaches. Even estuary fishing for snook is available in Laguna Coyuca.

Highlight Species

Sailfish, marlin, wahoo, dorado, pompano, yellowtail, barracuda, tuna, bonito, mackerel, snook, pargo, cabrilla, jacks, sierra.

Area Access

Acapulco's International Airport is accessed by Delta, American, Continental, Aeromexico, and Mexicana airlines. Considered the southernmost location of the Mexican Riviera resorts, Acapulco enjoys the direct service that Mexico Highway 200 provides. Cruise ships servicing the area include Carnival, Princess, Royal Caribbean, and Royal Viking.

Lodging, Camping/RV Options

The place is loaded with resorts of all price levels. Consider using the Hotel Mission, Suites Alba, Plaza las Glorias El Mirador, Hotel Los Flamingos, and Sol-I-Mar. Camping is prohibited in the Acapulco district. RV services are found north of town. Give the Quinta Dora Trailer Park a try.

Charters/Guide Service

The sportsfishing fleet at Acapulco is pretty extensive. Hotels can arrange for full services and rentals. Pangas and kayaks are available at the marina and along the waterfront. Give the following locations a try; Playa Caleta, Playa Hornos, and Barra Vieja.

JEFF SOLIS

Jeff Solis with a handsome yellowfin tuna.

The author with a chunky pargo colorado.

PUERTO ESCONDIDO

Fly Fishing Options

Inshore, offshore, rocky shore, estuary, and surf-zone options abound. Even though the area is well known as a travel destination, it hasn't developed the "mega" persona. Sportsfishing here is generally low-key but highly productive. The area is surrounded by six major rivers draining into the sea.

Highlight Species

Sailfish, marlin, dorado, pompano, yellowtail, barracuda, tuna, bonito, mackerel, pargo, cabrilla, jacks, sierra.

Area Access

Mexico Highway 200 takes you directly into the city. Puerto Escondido has an airport as well, however the flight schedule is strictly "inter-Mexico." Airlines servicing the town include Mexicana and Aerovias Oaxaquenas.

Lodging, Camping/RV Options

Try these recommended sites; Hotel Las Palmas, Hotel Rincon del Pacifico, Castillo de los Reyes, and the Cabañas Aldea. RV services can be found at the El Neptuno Trailer Park and the Puerto Escondido Trailer Park.

Charters/Guide Service

Pangas are available at Playa Principal. Charters can be arranged by most of the major hotels in town.

SANTA CRUZ/HUATULCO

Fly Fishing Options

This is probably my favorite fly-rodding locale in the entire region. It's untapped—wild—and a virtual fly-rod frontier screaming to be explored more thoroughly. Located in the Gulf of Tehuantepec, Bahias de Huatulco presents you with secluded coves, rocky structures, deep bays, and beautiful, idyllic beaches, which all add up to provide the highest quality fly-fishing adventure. Be sure to arrange for a boat to gain the best access throughout this magnificent arena.

Highlight Species

Sailfish, marlin, dorado, pompano, yellowtail, barracuda, tuna, bonito, mackerel, pargo, cabrilla, jacks, sierra.

Area Access

You can fly into the Huatulco International Airport with the following carriers; Mexicana Airlines and Aeromexico. A well-maintained secondary road off 200 provides access to Santa Cruz and the Bahia de Huatulco.

Lodging, Camping/RV Options

From Club Med to the Sheraton, this area is rapidly becoming a

ADVENTURES BEYOND IMAGES

favorite destination. Other lodging options include the Hotel Castillo Huatulco, Hotel Griffer, Posada Binniguenda, Suites Bugambilias, and Pasada del Padrino. RV campers can enjoy the Chahue Trailer Park. Camping on secluded beaches is a real option around the Huatulco area. The beaches are generally of the highest caliber.

Charters/Guide Service

Pangas are available in town and along the waterfront. For a full-service charter try Peterson's Odyssey. Charter services can be arranged at the larger resort hotels.

DAN BLANTON

Atwin King working tight to rocky structure.

PUERTO ARISTA

Fly Fishing Options

Surf zone and inshore options are your best chance for exploration. Sweeping beachheads and small barrier islands will provide most of the action.

Highlight Species

Pargo, cabrilla, jacks.

Area Access

Follow Highway 200 eastward, proceed past Juchitan and into the town of Tonala. Just south of Tonala, look for directions showing access to the village of Puerto Arista (approximately 10 miles to "PA"). The tiny Salina Cruz Airport is another option for folks traveling from Mexico City or Oaxaca. Aerovias Oaxaquenas provides the air service.

DAN BLANTON

A prized golden leopard grouper.

Lodging, Camping/RV Options

Don't expect a large selection for lodging in this area. Try the Hotel Puesta del Sol or the Hotel Bugambilias Arista. Camping is fine on the expansive beach. RV folks . . . you're on your own.

Charters/Guide Service

A charter service isn't available. Pangas can be rented along the beach.

Chapter EIGHT

Gulf Coast and Western Yucatán

Poling the flats near Campeche.

Henry Morgan was a seafaring man. He was a pirate by trade. Sure he got all the gold—but did he ever strike silver in the mangroves? I'm talking about tapping into those silver rockets that swarm the waters of Campeche and Champotón. The Gulf of Mexico's Western Yucatán Peninsula offers you an untapped resource for feisty tarpon and snook. It's a place where light-tackle fly fishing can reign supreme.

The area is home to a significant population of year-round resident tarpon. Larger migratory fish enter the bay and estuary system from October through January. The new arrivals are present, presumably to take advantage of the warmer waters and plentiful forage.

I had the good fortune to ply the flats and tidal creeks along the peninsula's western shoreline. It was a magnificent arena to puppeteer a streamer. I was presented with the options of casting over open flats, working amongst an entangled jungle, or casting along the banks of a large sinuous river. I reveled in all three! There's enough variety here to keep any fly fisher engaged.

My hosts to the area were Pepe Sansores and his son Jorge. For the past 55 years Pepe has made a living as the premiere guide for the region. His knowledge of the fisheries is an invaluable asset to anyone traveling to the area.

A massive mangrove jungle dominates the coastal habitat from Celestún down to Campeche. Campeche's charm lies in a series of extremely short river-corridors that bisect the jungle just north of town. Crystalline waters are the norm as each of the rivers empty into sweeping flats. The average depth here is typically two to five feet overall. The dynamics provide you with a perfect window to sight-fish. The estuary habitat was superb; shallow sandy-bottomed grass beds, banks dominated by mangrove roots, and a short channel or two created by the river's current.

The waterfront of Champoton.

GLENN KISHI

You can count on a wide variety of game fish to frequent the fertile territory. Tarpon, barracuda, snook, and even shark patrol the shallows searching for prey. It's a vintage setting to pursue the Yucatan's inshore fly-rodding game.

The estuary's open water affords the fly fisher 360 degrees of casting opportunity. Each of the river mouths averaged no more than 200 feet across. It was easy to cover their entire width with a few minor adjustments in boating position. Anyone would find it comfortable to cast to a cruising school of tarpon in this theater.

There's another game to play however, and I found it to be an additional pleasure of the region. It consists of an extensive system of narrow tidal creeks flowing deep into the mangrove jungle. The network of twisted channels and hidden pools harbored schools of tarpon and snook.

Searching the mangroves for silver kings.

As we traveled up the tidal creeks, they were literally just a few inches wider than the panga we piloted. Often both sides of the craft would simultaneously rub against the convoluted roots of the red mangrove trees. The technique for creeping along these waterways was a combination of poling, while at the same time grabbing the tree canopy for assistance. It was common to have the forest branches so low we had to kneel in the boat to gain passage. The mangrove jungle was a maze perfectly designed to protect its inhabitants. This adventure was total immersion for me. I relished the entrance into such an ancient place. The jungle's innermost sanctuary held secrets I wanted to uncover and understand. It was certainly worth the effort we put forth. There's no doubt in my mind that these ultra-close quarters aren't for everyone. It's quite the antithesis of the open-water game.

Fly fishing in these minute areas was the most demanding I've ever encountered. The intensely thick cover and micro habitat dictated altering our field technique drastically. Much of our success demanded a variety of short-cast applications. From steeple casts and side-arm presentations, to the bow-and-arrow and low-profiled roll-casts, you simply had to find a way to deliver your fly amidst tangles of greenery and wood. If you were lucky enough to have a clearing overhead, you still had to "thread the needle" on your back-cast before you could complete a presentation. Often we would incorporate a handy little trick from the steelheader's repertoire. We'd turn and face into the "backcast channel" and make that our forward stroke. The actual presentation of the fly would then happen on the reverse stroke.

We opted to work with small poppers in these tight quarters. The water was never deep and the fish would erupt on the fly just feet from our panga. Once the fly hit its mark we rarely got more than a three-strip retrieve. The game was indeed explosive and not for the faint of heart. I had one baby tarpon literally launch itself over the bow of the boat. I came unglued at the seams. I stood in awe with shredded nerves at the spectacle. I still shake my head today and smile at the tenacity of that silver rocket. I never did land it, the popper was never set, whew what a game!

South of Campeche, about an hour's drive, lies the Rio Champotón. This wide lazy river corridor offers about 20 miles of accessible tarpon territory. In addition to the tarpon, you might make time for targeting the snook, various jacks, snapper, and speckled trout in the river. The Rio Champotón is loaded with piscatorial delights.

The Rio Champotón system consists of three distinct flows merging somewhere in the heart of the Mayan Kingdom. The

Mangrove snapper are great fare for fly fishers.

Pangas aren't fancy . . . they're just highly effective.

tributaries must snake their way over 90 miles, through a jungle tapestry, before the river melds into the sea. The lower reaches are idyllic for fly fishing, offering clear flows and weather-protected habitat. This river will continue to produce excellent opportunities even if the northern waters of Campeche become blown out.

I've vivid memories from fly fishing the Rio Champotón. The site of hundreds of tarpon rolling within a 50-foot cast of my panga still gets my heart racing. I also remember watching a curtain of rain progress straight down the river, until the torrential downpour had engulfed us for merely a few brief moments and then vanished. That liquid curtain was all-consuming and seemed to suspend time. Then there is the prodigious egret rookery, moving as if it were a ballet of winged dancers as it assembled itself during the last rays of light. They were just a few moments from a treasure trove of countless prizes I value. The river was indeed a magical place to bring a fly rod. It was a place I found my spirit could soar.

Mexico's Gulf Coast and the Western Yucatán shoreline combine to offer you over 1,200 miles of adventurous fly-rodding. To the north, the region's woodland atmosphere houses bass in the Sierra Madre Oriental, while sea-trout and redfish make their respective residence among the Gulf's lagoons. Tuna and blue runner frequent the northern inshore environment. Traveling southward the atmosphere becomes much more tropical (particularly south of the Tropic of Cancer) with palm beaches, mangrove estuaries, rivers, and extensive inland jungles. Offshore, inshore, surf-zone, and estuary opportunities are almost limitless throughout the entire region. This lush sector provides you with a chance for everything from marlin and barracuda, to the kings of the coast, tarpon and snook.

Air travel to the Gulf and Western Yucatán is serviced by five airports. The following carriers provide the service; Mexicana and Aeromexico. You can arrange for connecting flights with a variety of carriers, especially Alaska Airlines and Aero California.

Tarpon cruising the Rio Champoton.

Land vehicles can access the region via Mexico Highway 180. Toll crossings become more of an issue as you travel below Tampico. The most common entry point is near Brownsville (Texas) at Matamoros. The road system is well-worn along this coast. A massive reconstruction project is currently being explored. Paved surfaces are typical even for the secondary routes of the region.

The hub cities along the Gulf of Mexico are Matamoros, Tampico, Tuxpan, Veracruz, and Villahermosa. Campeche is the hub for the Western Yucatán Peninsula.

This coastline includes the states of Tamaulipas, Veracruz, Tabasco, and Campeche.

MATAMOROS (AND SOUTHERN ENVIRONS)

Fly Fishing Options

Estuary, surf-zone, and inshore opportunities are best. The real action takes place quite a bit south of Matamoros proper. Two large barrier islands protect the shoreline environs. Four rivers intersect the state of Tamaulipas creating a well-defined series of lagoons and estuaries. San Fernando (65 miles south) is a great staging area to access these waters. The small fishing village of La Pesca (approximately 150 miles from Matamoros) provides the best inshore action. Largemouth are available inland at Lake Guerrero.

Highlight Species
Sea-trout, redfish, flounder, pargo, croaker, corvina, pompano, tuna, blue runner, tarpon, marlin, largemouth bass.

Area Access
Matamoros is the first town across the border, located along Mexico Highway 101/180. Its airport is serviced by Aeromexico. Secondary roads off 101/180 will provide access to the mouth of Laguna Madre, and farther south to San Fernando and the beaches of Playa Carbonera and Playa Carvajal. To get to the village of La Pesca, follow 180 south to Soto La Marina, where you exit (east) onto Mexico Highway 70 and proceed straight into the village. To reach Lake Guerrero, take 180 south of Matamoros until it branches off with Mexico Highway 70 (west). Follow 70 to Ciudad Victoria. Once in the city, ask for specific directions to the reservoir (it's about 20 miles from Victoria).

GLENN KISHI

Kurt Lemons tight to a silver king.

Lodging, Camping/RV Options
In Matamoros is the Hotel Roma, Hotel Ritz, and Hotel del Prado. Lodging in San Fernando is available at Motel La Serena, Motel La Hacienda, and Hotel Las Palomas. RVs can make their home at La Serena RV Park. Camping can be done almost anywhere you wish. Lodging around La Pesca includes El Refugio Motel, Hotel Villa del Mar, La Marina del Rio Campo Turista, and Campo la Pesca del Rio. RV access is at La Gaviota Trailer Park. Camping can be found on most of the resort properties. Lodging at Lake Guerrero includes Nuevo Padilla (off Highway 101), Villa de Casas (off Highway 70), Big Bass Lodge, and Club Exclusivo. RV parks include Hacienda Alta Vista, Campo El Sargento, El Pelicano, and La Tortuga.

Charters/Guide Service
Pangas are for hire along the waterfront at Matamoros, San Fernando, and La Pesca.

TAMPICO

Fly Fishing Options
Estuaries, flats, surf zone, inshore, offshore, and reservoir. The Carrizal and Tigre (San Rafael) rivers offer great estuary and flats fishing. Surf action can be found north of town and along the Barra del Tordo. A large reef, offshore from Barra del Tordo, can draw considerable action. North of Tampico, about 25 miles, is the town of Aldama (on the Rio Tigre). There is solid estuary fishing, as well as bass, in the small reservoir known as Presa Republica Espanola.

Glenn Kishi on assignment in a Yucatán jungle.

Highlight Species
Sea-trout, redfish, flounder, pompano, corvina, tarpon, snook, pargo, kingfish, tuna, marlin, largemouth bass.

Area Access
Driving south along Mexico Highway 180 provides the easiest route through the area. Paved and unimproved secondary roads provide direct access to remote beach locations. You can fly into Tampico Airport via Mexicana Airlines.

Lodging, Camping/RV Options
In Tampico there are the Jalisco, Tampico, and Inglaterra hotels. At Aldama is the Hotel Rancho Viejo, and El Paraiso Fishing and Hunting Lodge. Lodging at Barra del Tordo is limited, try the Hotel Playa Azul. Camping can be done pretty much anywhere you please.

Charters/Guide Service
Pangas are available at all waterfront locations. Charters are available out of Tampico.

TUXPAN

Fly Fishing Options
Estuary, surf zone, inshore, offshore. This is a major commercial fishing town. North of town is the extensive Laguna Tamiahua complete with interior islands. Outside the barrier is Cabo Rojo, with Isla Idolo and Isla Lobos. The Rio Tuxpan offers terrific estuary opportunities. Much farther south lies the Rio Tecolutla and excellent beach fishing.

Highlight Species
Tarpon, snook, sea-trout, redfish, croaker, jacks, tuna, marlin, kingfish.

Area Access
Drive south along Mexico Highway 180. There is a secondary route off 180 via Tamiahua and La Barra. To reach Playa Tecolutla, drive 45 miles south along 180.

Lodging, Camping/RV Options
Hotel Riviera, Hotel Sara, Hotel Reforma, and Hotel Florida. Camping is available at Playa Tuxpan. Lodging in Tecolutla includes Hotel Balneario Tecolutla and the Gran Hotel Playa MarSol.

Charters/Guide Service
Pangas are for hire along the waterfront. Charters are available at Aqua Sports Club Nautico de Buceo.

VERACRUZ

Fly Fishing Options
This site is the principal port on the Gulf. Heavy commercial traffic can be expected. Don't fret, a small trip to the outskirts of town will have you in great fishing waters. Beaches south of town include Mocambo and Boca del Rio. Jetty, surf-zone, inshore, and offshore opportunities are around the Veracruz area. Keep in mind that the entire state of Veracruz (from Tampico to the Rio Tonala) is laced with a multitude of river habitat. If you're adventurous and ambitious enough, you could explore a wealth of uncharted fly-fishing territory!

Highlight Species
Snook, sea-trout, redfish, croaker, jacks, tuna, marlin, kingfish.

Area Access

Continue south on 180. The Veracruz Airport is serviced by Mexicana Airlines.

Lodging, Camping/RV Options

Hotel Baluarte, Hotel Mar y Tierra, Hotel Playa Paraiso. The only RV park near Veracruz is the D.I.F. Balneario Mocambo Park.

Charters/Guide Service

Around the harbor you can find charters and pangas for hire. Try the Club de Yates Veracruz for more information.

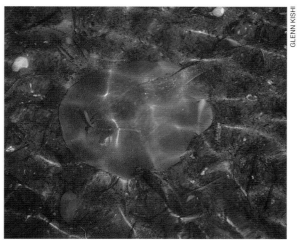

An unexpected beauty of the flats.

VILLAHERMOSA

This area is listed, in part, because of its airport access via Mexicana Airlines. Consider it a hub site to get supplies and rest a bit. It is not really recommended for its fly-fishing opportunities.

Lodging, Camping/RV Options

Hotel Don Carlos and Hotel Maya Tobasco.

CAMPECHE

Fly Fishing Options

Estuary, flats, river, and surf-zone habitats are available. The flats and massive mangrove system north of the city offer excellent shots at tarpon and snook. South of Campeche in the village of Champotón, you can explore protected riverine habitat plus the surf-zone prospects.

Highlight Species

Tarpon, snook, barracuda, jacks, sea-trout.

Area Access

Located directly on Mexico Highway 180. The Campeche Airport is serviced by Aeromexico.

Lodging, Camping/RV Options

Try the Hotel Baluartes and Ramada Inn at Campeche. RV campers can use the Campeche Trailer Park. Lodging at Champotón is best at the Snook Inn.

Charters/Guide Service

Pangas can be hired along the waterfronts of Campeche and Champotón.

You guessed it, tarpon are a wild ride.

Chapter NINE

Northern Yucatán and Caribbean Coasts

It is a place where Gulf waters meld into the Caribbean's warmer realm. Large predators proliferate in the area as they travel with maritime currents. The Yucatán Peninsula's northern coastline provides a wondrous setting for exploring these rich offshore waters.

In contrast to the peninsula's northern environs, its southern Caribbean coastline is a Mecca for stalking bonefish and permit. No other area offers you such expansive flats for this unique pursuit. The region's sparkling waters have rapidly become legend in the fly fishing community. The locations of the flats are remote, protected, and teeming with game.

Large barrier reefs provide the shallows with protection from the open ocean's swells. The area's Palancar Reef is one of the world's largest such environments. The monumental structure and its fertile waters are chock-full of life. Palancar's unique habitat provides world-class fly-rodding opportunities.

The Northern Yucatán and Caribbean coasts snake around Mexico's easternmost peninsula. Combined, they represent about 1,000 miles of uninterrupted shoreline. Waters from the Gulf of Mexico lap against the western and northern shores. The peninsula's eastern shoreline is caressed by the Caribbean Sea.

The interior of the peninsula is comprised of scrub-like desert mixed with thick stands of tropical jungle. There isn't much in the way of rivers or streams. Most of the water percolates down through the soil and becomes subterranean in nature.

This is a land of mystical and mythical influence, both in cultures past and present. The Mayan civilization created a powerful presence still felt as you travel the region today. Their preference in architecture, their insights on science, and certainly their relationship to the natural world around them continues to inspire new inhabitants of the peninsula.

Ralph and Lisa Cutter have a thirst for adventure. I can appreciate their excitement of "unexpected events." I've asked Ralph to convey one of those moments during a recent trip into the Yucatán. The following story is in Ralph's own words.

By mid-morning the heat, humidity, and mosquitoes began taking their toll. We doggedly pressed on until the boat could be dragged no further, then we slogged upstream through calf-deep mud for another 30 minutes. Choc pointed to a small brook trickling out of the undergrowth. With a wave of the machete and with a gleam in his eye he asked, "¿Listo?"

A few steps into the jungle and we came face to face with a Mayan ruin lost amid a dense tangle of roots and vines. The quiet sound of an artesian spring bubbling at the entrance and the dappled light playing on the structure gave the setting a palpable tranquillity. The temple had aged gracefully and seemed as much a part of the jungle as the river, the trees, and birds. Choc revealed a small penlight and as a light rain began to fall, we ducked inside.

The first room was the size of an American kitchen but the ceiling forced us to stoop. The walls were of limestone blocks and roots crawled through the cracks like octopus arms groping for unseen prey. The air was thick and still. It smelled of clean dirt. A half dozen tittering bats wheeled

Lisa Cutter with her hands full in Boca Paila.

RALPH CUTTER

and darted through the gloom and into portals leading deeper. We followed the bats through a series of small rooms and into near darkness.

By the beam of the penlight, Choc plowed the loamy soil with his machete. Small shards of pottery and bits of shell were quickly fingered and tossed aside. While Choc excavated, Lisa and I examined the carvings on the walls. The forms of birds, snakes, and fish could be clearly deciphered amid the seemingly random shapes and designs. Lisa found a perfect carving of an alligator and pointed it out to Choc. He asked, "Would you like it?" Lisa said no and I backed her decision by telling Choc I thought it was better left where it was. Choc tackled the carving anyway and started prying the block away from the wall. Again we told him we didn't want it but still he continued to pry.

We started feeling uneasy about the whole thing. This was a special and beautiful place and to desecrate it was obviously wrong. Imperceptibly the room grew damp and cold. Our feelings of excitement and adventure were replaced by foreboding. I sensed that Choc was feeling less exuberant about the whole thing too. As the block loosened, it unleashed a torrent of dirt and rock and filled the room with choking dust.

As bats swirled in the dust a crisp whirring sound welled in the darkness. "¡Cascabel!" Choc cried out and we chased him on all fours as he bolted out of the room. Pressed against the wall of the "kitchen" room was a gorgeous central American rattlesnake as thick as my calf. Ropy coils looped against the roots and the rattle blurred. We gave it wide berth and scuttled out the door and into the brightness. Within seconds we were soaked to the bone by a cold tropical rain.

It was early evening when we poled the boat out of the creek and into the lagoon. The squall had moved on, leaving a faint rainbow and an aftermath of pink and orange clouds. The mangroves glistened with rain drops and the water was as flat and calm as a sheet of glass. A moon-like permit quietly tailed amid a pencil garden of mangrove shoots. It felt like a surreal dream.

I glanced down at the fly rod and smiled; some things are better left the way they are.

In 1986, the Mexican government declared part of the Quintana Roo region a unique reserve. Unlike any other national park, the Sian Ka'an Biosphere Reserve represents a new concept in "protected land management." It's a massive biosphere encompassing more than 1 million acres of varied habitat and wildlife communities. The reserve represents one of the single largest protected areas in the world. This jewel of nature houses tropical jungles, mangrove swamps, beachheads, flats, and coral reefs. It also protects significant archaeological sites. In 1987 the Sian Ka'an project was named a World Heritage Site by UNESCO.

Traveling to, and through, the Northern Yucatán and Caribbean coasts can be easy. Air transportation will bring you directly to the hub cities of Mérida, Cancún, and Cozumel. Carriers include Mexicana, Aeromexico, Aerocaribe, American, United, and Continental airlines.

Driving the region you'll find the most extensive access provided by Mexico Highways 180, 186, and 307. Highway 180 follows the "Gulf Coast" and continues north into Mérida. It then cuts eastward across the Peninsula's northern tip to Puerto Juarez and the Cancún environs. Highway 186 originates in Villahermosa. It will provide you with a southern access to Highway 307 and the Caribbean coastline.

Cruise ships also frequent the ports of Cancún and Cozumal. Royal Caribbean, Norwegian Caribbean, and Carnival Cruise lines provide the service.

The states of Yucatán and Quintana Roo comprise this sector of Mexico. The small country of Belize lies immediately south of the Quintana Roo region.

John Shewey releases another "flats wolf". . . a great barracuda!

Lisa Cutter caught this hefty jack on a crab pattern.

Juan with Xavier Carbonet exploring Ascension Bay backcountry.

RALPH CUTTER

CELESTÚN

Fly Fishing Options

Inshore and estuary habitats are key here. The surf zone is another option you might wish to explore. Celestún is located at the southern tip of a crescent peninsula. The protected waters offer a classic estuary environment. Celestún actually houses a nature preserve, The National Center for the Study of Aquatic Birds, with over 200 species including the beautiful flamingo. Just south of the peninsula lies an extensive mangrove jungle well worth exploring.

Highlight Species

Tarpon, snook, barracuda, jacks, ladyfish, and croaker.

Area Access

Take Mexico Highway 180 into the hub city of Mérida. At the northern end of the city look for the junction leading west toward the settlements of Sisal and Celestún. The drive from Mérida is approximately 60 miles. Licenciado Manuel Crescencio Rejon International Airport, located in Mérida, is the central site for air traffic.

Lodging, Camping/RV Options

There isn't much in Celestún. Campers and RV travelers are on your own. Your best bet for lodging is to stay in Mérida and day-trip to the coast.

Charters/Guide Service

Pangas are available on the waterfront.

MÉRIDA

Fly Fishing Options

Located inland, this is more of a "central headquarters" for the region. The capital city will provide you with access to the entire Yucatán Peninsula. Immediate areas on the northern coastline include Celestún, Sisal, and Progreso. Of particular interest is the inshore environs of Arrecife Sisal and Arrecife Madagascar. The surf zone and inshore habitat around Progreso can be very productive. Again, Celestún's environs offer terrific estuary habitat.

Highlight Species

Tuna, bonito, tarpon, snook, jacks, barracuda, and pargo.

Area Access

Licenciado Manuel Crescencio Rejon International Airport is serviced by the following carriers; Aeromexico, Mexicana, Aerocaribe, Continental, and American airlines. Mexico Highway 180 is the main road system into Mérida.

Lodging, Camping/RV Options

Recommended sites include the Grant Hotel, Mérida Mission Park Inn, María del Carmen, and Los Aluxes. RV campers can find services at the Rainbow Trailer Park.

Charters/Guide Service

If you haven't already made these plans with your travel agent, you'll need to arrange for the services at the individual destinations you plan to visit.

ISLA MUJERES

Fly Fishing Options

Inshore and offshore opportunities are strong options from this location. Surf zone and rocky shore habitat are also available around the island.

Highlight Species

Kingfish, sailfish, marlin, mackerel, bonito, barracuda, jacks, snapper, and bonefish.

Area Access

Unless you have a private boat, you'll be using the public ferry service. Just north of Cancún you'll find two services available; the car ferry leaves from Punta Sam, where the passenger-only ferry originates at Puerto Juarez.

Lodging, Camping/RV Options

Plenty to choose from; Posada del Mar, Perla del Caribe 2, Cabañas María del Mar, Hotel Caribe Maya, Hotel Cristalmar.

Charters/Guide Service

Hotel management will be happy to arrange these services for you.

CANCÚN CITY AND ISLA CANCÚN

Fly Fishing Options

Inshore, offshore, surf zone, and flats habitat are all options around the fabled Cancún environs. Try working the waters around Playa Las Perlas, Playa Tortugas, and Playa Chac-Mool.

Highlight Species

Kingfish, sailfish, marlin, mackerel, bonito, barracuda, jacks, snapper, and bonefish.

Area Access

Mexico Highway 180 takes you directly to Cancún from Mérida. Drivers from the south would first use Mexico Highway 186 toward Chetumal, eventually taking Mexico Highway 307 directly up the Caribbean Coast to Cancún. Cancún International Airport offers flight service for Mexicana, Aeromexico, Aerocaribe, American, Continental, and United airlines.

Lodging, Camping/RV Options

The Sheraton Cancún, Cancún Marriott, Club Lagoon, Hotel Aristos, Days Inn El Pueblito, and Plaza del Sol are all fine choices. RV campers should try the Rainbow Trailer Park.

Charters/Guide Service

There is an extensive fleet of charters and skiffs available. You can hire boats right at the marinas or let your hotel make the necessary arrangements for you.

PUERTO MORELOS AND PUNTA BETE

Fly Fishing Options

Inshore and surf zone habitats dominate the area. Offshore opportunities are possible. This stretch of the Caribbean Coast is still pretty much undeveloped and can be a pleasant getaway from the larger resorts. Fly-fishers afoot will enjoy the terrific beaches here.

Highlight Species

Kingfish, sailfish, marlin, mackerel, bonito, barracuda, jacks, snapper.

Area Access

These two locations lie south of Cancún on Mexico Highway 307. Puerto Moralos is about 20 miles down the highway. Punta Bete is another 18 miles or so. The tiny hamlet is actually accessed by a secondary road off "307." It is easy to miss the sign that takes you onto the unimproved road. Keep in mind the exit is roughly a few miles north of Playa del Carmen.

Ralph Cutter with an Ascension Bay tarpon.

LISA CUTTER

Lodging, Camping/RV Options

In Puerto Moralos try the Posada Amor. At Punta Bete use La Posada del Capitán Lafitte or the Cabañas Xcalacoco. Camping and RV options can be found near the Cabañas as well.

Charters/Guide Service

Check with the dive shops in each location.

PLAYA DEL CARMEN

Fly Fishing Options

Inshore and surf zone habitats are key. Offshore excursions can be possible.

Highlight Species

Kingfish, sailfish, marlin, mackerel, bonito, barracuda, jacks, snapper.

Area Access

The village is located directly off Mexico Highway 307.

Lodging, Camping/RV Options

Hotel Molcas, Hotel Delfin, Coast del Mar, Cabañas Nuevo Amanecer, Hotel Playa del Carmen, and the Blue Parrot Inn. Camping is great in the area. Be sure to try Camping Las Ruinas. North of town, RV services are available at Playa Xcalacoco Campground.

Charters/Guide Service

The local dive shop could help with arrangements.

COZUMEL

Fly Fishing Options

Inshore and offshore opportunities are abundant around the island. Cozumel's shoreline is part of an extensive underwater preserve, and as such, angling from shore is prohibited.

Highlight Species

Kingfish, sailfish, marlin, mackerel, bonito, barracuda, jacks, snapper.

Area Access

Cozumel International Airport is serviced by Mexicana, American Airlines, and Aerocaribe. Ferry service is conducted from Playa del Carmen and Puerto Morelos. Standard passenger service is available at the Playa del Carmen terminal.

Lodging, Camping/RV Options

Villas Las Anclas, Howard Johnson Casa del Mar, Hotel Vista del Mar, Melia Mayan Cozumel, and Sol Cabañas del Caribe. Camping is very limited; try around Playa Chen Rio or Punta Ciquero.

Charters/Guide Service

It is easiest to have your hotel take care of the arrangements.

PAAMUL AND AKUMAL

Fly Fishing Options

Outstanding offshore, inshore, and rocky shore opportunities are found around here. Surf zone options can produce some exciting action as well.

Highlight Species

King mackerel, dorado, sailfish, marlin, bonito, barracuda, jacks, snapper.

Area Access

Direct access is provided by Mexico Highway 307. Paamul is about 55 miles south of Cancún. Akumal is another 10 miles south of Paamul.

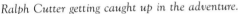

Ralph Cutter getting caught up in the adventure.

LISA CUTTER

Lodging, Camping/RV Options
In Paamul use the Hotel Paamul and Trailer Park. In Akumal try the Zacil Bungalows, Club Akumal Caribe Villas Maya, or Hotel Akumal Cancún.

Charters/Guide Service
Pangas available on the waterfront. Dive shops here can be a great help for booking services.

BOCA PAILA PENINSULA

Fly Fishing Options
This 22-mile strip represents the northernmost border of the Sian Ka'an Biosphere Reserve. Flats and estuary options are the key habitats to this area. Inshore waters are also an option.

Highlight Species
Bonefish, permit, tarpon, barracuda, snook, mackerel, dorado, sailfish, marlin, bonito, jacks, snapper.

Area Access
Take Mexico Highway 307. South of Tulum follow the secondary road leading down the peninsula.

Lodging, Camping/RV Options
Near the Tulum Ruins try Cabañas Don Armando, Cabañas Chac-Mool, and Cabañas Tulum. Boca Paila Fishing Lodge is located on Laguna Paila. Informal camping and RV services can be found along the peninsula.

Charters/Guide Service
The best services are provided at Boca Paila Fishing Lodge.

ASCENSIÓN BAY (AND ESPÍRITU SANTO BAY)

Fly Fishing Options
Ascensión Bay is located in the heart of the Sian Ka'an Biosphere Reserve. Espíritu Santo is closer to the southern environs. Spectacular flats and reef fishing opportunities exist in both bays. The Palancar Reef rivals Australia's Great Barrier Reef. The extensive mangrove estuaries in Ascensión Bay and the Espíritu Santo region are pretty much unchartered treasure chests.

Highlight Species
Bonefish, permit, tarpon, barracuda, snook, mackerel, dorado, sailfish, marlin, bonito, jacks, snapper.

Area Access
Off of Mexico Highway 307, follow the road that leads down the Boca Paila Peninsula. The unimproved road ends at Punta Allen. Don't be in a hurry. It represents over a three-hour drive from Cancún. Boat shuttles from Punta Allen or private air taxis from Cancún, are the only access into Casa Blanca Lodge and the central bay region.

Lodging, Camping/RV Options
Cuzan Lodge (at Punta Allen) and Casa Blanca Lodge (Punta Pájaros). Since there is no road system around the bay environs, camping and RV opportunities aren't realistic.

Charters/Guide Service
Outstanding services are provided by the lodges.

Chapter TEN

The Baja Peninsula

The pangero was heading his skiff around the southern tip of Isla del Carmen. The straight between Isla Danzante to the west, and Punta Baja to the east, was erupting with bonito slashing through balls of sardines. It was just the sight I was hoping to see.

Rafael saw the raining bait far before I had picked it up. He was already swinging the bow of the panga toward the edge of the boils. He cut the power to the engine, far enough from the frenzy, to slide within 50 feet of the feeding zone. We were positioned slightly up-current with a mild drift taking affect. Rafael used a rough-hewn sculling paddle to fine-tune the skiff's position.

On my first cast I was tight to a bonehead. That very fish decided to take me to school right then and there. It was the first Sea of Cortez bonito I'd ever taken and didn't realize the heat they could generate. I mean almost instantaneous heat! The line was ripping through my stripping hand and smoking my fingers. I was so taken aback by the fish's strength, it took a moment to release my grip on the line and get the fish onto the reel. It was truly a struggle to concentrate on the bonito and not give in to my burning fingers. I didn't know whether to cheer from excitement or scream from the searing pain.

DAN BLANTON

Trey Combs, Dan Blanton, Steve Abel, and Ed Givens discuss patterns.

The bonito blasted straight from the pack and had me into my backing within seconds. Just as I was coming under control a large bill broke through the surface. I felt a tremendous jolt race through the rod and then—nothing. My bonito had just been ripped by a marlin. Rafael sported a grin from ear to ear. I stood on the bow deck completely in shock. Man, what an awesome welcome to the world of "Cortez fly rodding."

A decade later it was my pleasure to host Ed DiGardi on his first Baja saltwater adventure. Where'd we go? I took him to that sweet spot where I'd been burned by the infamous bonehead. With our skiff heading toward Punta Baja, we were treated to the same wonderful scene of schooling bonito and raining bait.

This time, instead of concentrating on the bones we opted to round the point and work along Isla del Carmen's eastern flank. It was predawn and the Sea of Cortez was as calm as a pond. The welcoming committee was comprised of acrobatic rays, more hungry bonito, and surface-sunning billfish. We had hoped to find rafting sargasso or some other form of floating cover, and the accompanying schools of dorado. We never found the floating cover, but we did find the dorado.

At one point our panga was surrounded by escaping bait. The dorado were lit up and slashing from all directions. The magnificent green and gold wolves were ravenous hunters. It was pure rapture with a fly rod. Streamers were devoured on every cast. Poppers were taken with reckless abandon. The competition between dorado hit a feverish pitch. Ed was both wide-eyed and wired. His fingertips were raw. I smiled to myself as I witnessed another awesome introduction to the Cortez game.

The fly-fishing community owes much to the hearty adventurers who first had the vision to cast into the blue Sea of Cortez. With little more than a wanderlust spirit and a passion for saltwater game fish, players like Harry Kime, Dan Blanton, Nick Curcione, and Bob Edgley began to pave the way to Baja's rich resources. Collectively they've been an inspiration to me and a catalyst for initiating my own explorations of Baja's coastal habitat.

More recently the adventure of Baja fly fishing has been extended to include the utterly vast world of "blue water." Now commonly referred to as off-shore, or long-range excursions. Pioneers such as Trey Combs and Ray Beadle have taken the art of saltwater fly rodding to a new level. The fly-fisher's realm just continues to expand and inspire.

The Baja is wild. It's nature in the raw. It's a great place for a fly rod! Two states, Baja Norte and Baja Sur, combine to create the longest peninsula in the world. The entire coastline presents just under 2,000 miles of fantasy fly fishing. The only true way to completely access the coastal environs is via boat. However, land access is pretty extensive and provides more possibilities than most people could explore in a lifetime.

The western shore is sculpted by the Pacific's powerful forces. Kelp beds, offshore pinnacles and seastacks, numerous large bays, and huge estuary systems are characteristic of the Baja's west coast personality. Crossing over the high desert plateau to the peninsula's eastern shore, you'll discover its features impacted by the warmer Sea of Cortez (Gulf of California). Craggy promontories,

DAN BLANTON

Nancy Morris with a marlin off Thetis Bank.

Fully rigged and ready to go for offshore action.

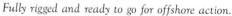

RAY BEADLE

Walt Jennings releases a striped marlin.

RAY BEADLE

GLENN KISHI

Two great color schemes for inshore poppers.

small bays, and an abundance of island habitat typifies this remote coastline.

Baja's northern interior is dominated by four mountain chains. In the Sierra San Pedro Martir you'll discover terrain much like California's Sierra Nevada range. The wild Rio Santo Domingo and a few of its tributaries even harbor beautiful rainbow trout.

Baja's southern interior is a wasteland in fly-fishing terms. Along the eastern peninsula is the impressive Sierra de la Giganta. In the southernmost region, the Sierra del Laguna lords over the land.

Air travel to the Baja is provided by Aero California, Aeromexico, Mexicana, and Alaska airlines. Baja Norte has a single airport located in Tijuana. Baja Sur is serviced by airports in Loreto, La Paz, and San Jose del Cabo (Cabo San Lucas).

The Transpeninsula Highway (Mexico Highway 1) is the main access on the west coast. It travels the coastline to El Rosario then ventures eastward along the northern interior. At Parador it splits, with the eastern leg terminating on the Sea of Cortez at Bahia de Los Angeles. The western leg continues south, back to the coast and on to Guerrero Negro. At this point, the highway turns to the east once again, heading to Santa Rosalia, and onward down the Cortez coastline to Loreto. The Transpeninsula Highway ultimately travels south to La Paz, San Jose del Cabo, and terminates at Cabo San Lucas.

There's another main access route in the northeastern sector. Mexico Highway 5 travels from the border, near Mexicali, south into San Felipe. Northern Baja travelers can also traverse the extreme northern locales along Mexico Highway 2, ultimately crossing onto the Mexican mainland, into the state of Sonora.

Hub cities in Baja Norte include Rosarito, Enseñada, San Felipe, and San Quintin. Baja Sur offers Santa Rosalia, Loreto, La Paz, and Cabo San Lucas. Even though we have identified eight key sites, the Baja Peninsula hosts numerous towns, fishing camps, and settlements. Many can be found in rather remote locations throughout the entire peninsula. It's to your advantage to further explore the countryside.

Cruise lines also service Baja's territory. Enseñada (northern Baja) and the Los Cabos (southern Baja) areas are the ports-o-call.

ROSARITO (AND SOUTHERN ENVIRONS)

Fly Fishing Options
Surf zone, kelp beds, inshore. The beach habitat is extensive in the area. The sand quality is medium to fine grain and perfect for housing perch and corbina food. The kelp beds are extremely close to shore and within easy reach of a kayak or cartop skiff.

Highlight Species
Barred surfperch, corbina, flatfish, opaleye, calico bass, sand bass, rockfish, Pacific barracuda, and croaker.

Area Access
Driving your own rig, simply follow the newly renovated Mexico Highway 1-D (toll road). Or, you can follow the older Tijuana/Enseñada free road (Mexico 1). Direct coastal access is via

most secondary roads. Another option for travel around this region is flying into Tijuana and renting a vehicle. Fishing villages of particular interest would include the following locales; Popotla, Santa Martha, Puerto Nuevo, and Canta Mar.

Lodging, Camping/RV Options
Lodging and RV camps abound in this sector. Try the Rosarito Beach Hotel or Los Pelicanos Hotel in town. South onto Puerto Nuevo is the Hotel New Port Baja and the Grand Baja Resort. RV and camping options include the KOA facility just north of Rosarito, and numerous small operations in most of the villages south. Camping within the confines of the Rosarito city limits is illegal.

Charters/Guide Service
Pangas are available for hire along the waterfront of most fishing villages.

ENSEÑADA

Fly Fishing Options
Offshore, inshore, kelp and rocky shore, surf zone, and estuary. The Bahia de Todos Santos is home port for a large sportsfishing industry. Everything from long-range vessels to local panga rentals are available. The rocky shores and kelp beds around Punta Banda are perfect for fly-fishers working from small skiffs. The Isla de Todos Santos is another productive site accessible by skiff. Anglers on foot can explore the surf, particularly the Estero Beach environs, or cast from the rocks near La Bufadora. Long-range operations can take anglers to the far reaches of the entire coast (and beyond).

Highlight Species
Calico bass, sand bass, perch, opaleye, Pacific barracuda, rockfish, bonita, mackerel, yellowtail, white sea bass, tuna, wahoo, marlin.

Area Access
Mexico route Highway 1-D, and the older Highway 1, are both available taking you directly into Enseñada. Again, coastal access is via unimproved and paved secondary roadways. There is a small airport in Enseñada completely capable of servicing private aircraft. Starlite Cruises and the Royal Caribbean Line provide cruise ship service to this international port.

Lodging, Camping/RV Options
Lodging in Enseñada includes The San Nicolas, Villa Fontana, and Hotel La Pinta. Camping is good at Playa San Miguel, Playa Hermosa, and Playa el Faro. RV parks are best south of town near Maneadero and the Punta Banda peninsula. Try Estero Beach Trailer Park, La Jolla Beach Camp, and Villarino RV Park (which has pangas for rent as well).

Charters/Guide Service
A wide variety of charters and skiffs are for hire in the Enseñada harbor. You can find many of them located at the Federalson Sportfishing Landing.

SAN FELIPE

Fly Fishing Options
Surf zone and inshore opportunities are best in the area from San Felipe to Puertecitos. North of San Felipe are a series of remote estuaries worth exploring. Ask for directions to Boca la Bolsa.

Del Brown caught this blue star off Southern Baja's coast (circa 1975).

DAN BLANTON

The panga fleet at Loreto.

Highlight Species
Sierra, corvina, white sea bass, cabrilla, sand bass, triggerfish, pargo, croaker, and flatfish.

Area Access
There is direct access from the east on Mexico Highway 5. Western travelers will have to traverse the Baja, either from Tijuana via Mexico Highway 2, or from Enseñada via BCN-16 until it connects with Highway 5 at San Felipe. To access the upper estuaries you'll need 4-wheel-drive capabilities once you exit the main highway. The road leading south from San Felipe to Puertecitos is unimproved but accessible for two-wheel-drive vehicles.

Lodging, Camping/RV Options
In San Felipe try the El Capitán Motel and Motel el Cortes. RV parks include Mar del Sol, Rubin's Trailer Park, and Playa de Laura Trailer Park.

Charters/Guide Service
Both charters and pangas can be hired in town.

SAN QUINTIN

Fly Fishing Options
Surf zone, estuary, and inshore opportunities available. This area has an expansive bay and estuary system. The beaches along Bahia de San Quintin are excellent. Isla San Martín and local seamounts, such as Roca Ben, offer great inshore prospects.

Highlight Species
Barred perch, calico bass, rockfish, sand bass, flatfish, yellowtail, bonito, Pacific barracuda, and tuna.

Area Access

Mexico Highway 1 is the only way to reach San Quintin. Unimproved secondary roads provide direct access to the coast.

Lodging, Camping/RV Options

Old Mill Motel and Ernesto's Resort Motel are your best bets on the bay. South of San Quintin, on Playa Santa María, is the more modern Hotel La Pinta. Camping is best along Playa Pabellon. RV facilities are available at Campo de Lorenzo and Honey's RV Campground.

Charters/Guide Service

Pangas are available at the motels and RV parks mentioned. There are currently no commercial charters for hire.

SANTA ROSALIA (AND SOUTHERN ENVIRONS)

Fly Fishing Options

Rocky shore, inshore, offshore, and surf zone environments can be explored. Crags and coves offer tremendous habitat for anglers on foot or afloat. Isla San Marcos and Isla Tortuga present inshore anglers with a highly productive zone. Heading a bit south, the beaches around Punta Chivato are superb.

Highlight Species

Yellowtail, dorado, tuna, marlin, bonito, sierra, cabrilla, pargo, triggerfish, sand bass, leopard grouper, corvina, ladyfish, and flatfish.

Area Access

Continue your drive along Mexico Highway 1, crossing the peninsula's interior. Mexico Highway 1 will take you directly into Santa Rosalia. Unimproved and paved secondary roads provide direct access to the Sea of Cortez coastline.

Lodging, Camping/RV Options

Hotel El Morro and Hotel del Real are good choices in Santa Rosalia. South of town is the San Lucas RV Park. Camping is good along most beaches in the area. Lodging at Punta Chivato is pretty remote, try the Hotel Punta Chivato.

Charters/Guide Service

Charters and pangas are for hire at the marina in Santa Rosalia. Pangas can be hired on the waterfront around Punta Chivato.

LORETO

Fly Fishing Options

Inshore, offshore, rocky shore, and surf zone. The Loreto area is one of the most famous fly-rodding destinations in Baja. The islands of Carmen, Danzante, and Coronado are magnets for a wide variety of game fish. The beaches and jetties around Loreto are an untapped pleasure. Offshore anglers will find plenty of big-game action in the region.

Highlight Species

Dorado, roosterfish, yellowtail, tuna, marlin, bonito, skipjack, sierra, cabrilla, leopard grouper, pargo, triggerfish, sand bass, corvina, ladyfish.

Area Access

Mexico Highway 1 is all you need to drive. The Loreto Airport is serviced by Aero California.

RAY BEADLE

Trey Combs with a record wahoo.

Kelp beds dominate Baja's northern coastline.

Lodging, Camping/RV Options
The Hotel La Pinta, Hotel Oasis, La Mision Hotel, and The Presidente are great choices. Loreto's Tripui RV Park is a fine resource.

Charters/Guide Service
Charters and pangas are available through the hotels. Pangas can also be hired along the waterfront at the marinas.

LA PAZ

Fly Fishing Options
Offshore, inshore, rocky shore and surf zone areas available. This is a major sportfishing zone, with inshore and offshore pursuits dominating the game. The islands of Espiritu Santo, Partida, and Cerralvo are famous for their big-game appeal.

Highlight Species
Dorado, roosterfish, yellowtail, tuna, marlin, bonito, sierra, cabrilla, pargo, triggerfish, sand bass.

Area Access
Mexico Highway 1 takes you directly into La Paz. Secondary roads leaving town let you explore a variety of beaches. Aero California and Aeromexico both service the La Paz airport.

Lodging, Camping/RV Options
Lodging in town includes El Mason, Los Arcos, Hotel Perla, and Hotel Gardenias. The Oasis Los Aripez is a great RV park.

Charters/Guide Service
Charters and pangas are available for hire. Most hotels can help you arrange the services.

CABO SAN LUCAS

Fly Fishing Options
Offshore, inshore, rocky shore and surf zone areas available.

"Lawrence of Loreto" Digardi with a hot schoolie dorado.

Highlight Species
Marlin, dorado, roosterfish, wahoo, yellowtail, tuna, bonito, sierra, cabrilla, pargo, triggerfish, sand bass.

Area Access
The Transpeninsula Highway terminates at Cabo San Lucas (Land's End). Los Cabos Airport, located north of Cabo near Santa Anita, is serviced by Alaska Airlines, Aero California, and Mexicana Airlines. The following cruise lines provide service to the area; Princess, Royal Caribbean, and Carnival.

Lodging, Camping/RV Options
Solmar Suites, Hotel Marina, Finisterra, Melia San Lucas, and

Corbina are a real test for surf-zone anglers.

Hotel Hacienda are great resources. The Vagabundos Trailer Park is located a few miles north of Cabo.

Charters/Guide Service
Any motel can help arrange charter and panga services. The Cabo marinas are home port to some of the most famous fleets in Mexico.

TWO BONUS LOCATIONS...

RIO SANTO DOMINGO

Fly Fishing Options
Remote mountain streams located in Sierra San Pedro Martir range. The populations of fish aren't widespread, but are very healthy.

Highlight Species
Rainbow trout. First documented in the Santo Domingo river system during a 1908 expedition. During more recent times the fishery has been managed by private concessionaire.

Area Access
My first encounter with Baja trout took place during a backpacking session in Parque Nacional Sierra San Pedro Martir. The fish were caught in the Rio San Rafael drainage. The going could be rough if you're not in condition to handle this rugged backcountry. Another option is to take full advantage of a wonderful horsepacking adventure with commercial outfitters.

Charters/Guide Service
The horsepacking service is provided by Enrique Meling and his staff at Meling Adventures.

ADVENTURES BEYOND IMAGES

Fresh sardina baitfish are a real boost for attracting action.

BAHIA MAGDALENA

Fly Fishing Options
Offshore, inshore, estuary, and surf-zone environments abound. This is one of the most awesome estuary systems I've ever explored with a fly rod. Mangrove creeks, deep channels, open bays, barrier islands, isolated beaches all provide wonderful opportunities for a variety of game fish. Inshore prospects are outstanding around the area's many islands. Offshore locales are famous for their consistent big-game action.

Highlight Species
Spotted sand bass, broomtail grouper, cabrilla, flatfish, pompano, corvina, sierra, barred perch, yellowtail, wahoo, marlin.

Area Access
Take Mexico Highway 1 south into Ciudad Constitucíon. From town take the paved road west to San Carlos (BC-4 also known as Mexico Highway 22). Another access is via Highway 1, heading south from Constitucíon to Santa Rita. From Santa Rita take the unimproved road west to Puerto Chale, which is simply a tiny fishing camp.

Lodging, Camping/RV Options
Lodging and supplies are best in Ciudad Constitucíon. San Carlos has a small motel and limited support. Puerto Chale has no support services. You can camp/RV most anywhere. . . but beware of the bugs!

Charters/Guide Service
Pangas are available in San Carlos. You can also arrange for pangas in the lodging of Ciudad Constitucíon. San Carlos has the only launch ramp accessible for larger craft.

Harry Kime with a Coronado Island yellowtail (circa 1970).

DAN BLANTON

Chapter ELEVEN
Fly Patterns and Recipes

The following patterns have a proven track record in Mexican waters. Their combined presence addresses the needs for surf zone, estuary and flats, rocky shore and kelp, inshore, and offshore adventures. Instead of recounting which species was caught on which fly, I have found it more useful to point out which habitats will match each pattern.

By no means is this collection all-inclusive. The 32 patterns chosen represent a great starting point for assembling your own selections. As fly designers learn more about the natural history of the predator/prey relationships down south, I've no doubt that excellent patterns will continue to evolve.

Apte Too Plus, or Black Death

Hook:	2-2/0.
Thread:	Red.
Tail Support:	Monofilament, create a loop extended from rear of shank.
Tail:	Black rabbit strip. Add a few strands of flash per side.
Collar:	Squirrel tail, dyed red.
Head:	Red thread.
Optics:	Painted eyes, white/black pupil.
Suggested Uses:	Estuary and flats.

Baja Streaker

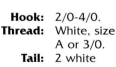

Hook:	2/0-4/0.
Thread:	White, size A or 3/0.
Tail:	2 white saddle hackles per side. A few strands of silver flash per side.
Ribbing:	Silver wire, medium.
Body:	Pearl Mylar.
Wing:	Matching set of peacock swords.
Throat and Cheeks:	White bucktail for throat. Yellow bucktail for cheeks.
Head and Optics:	Tying thread. Solid plastic doll eyes; medium, silver/black pupil.
Suggested Uses:	Inshore and offshore.

Balsa Popper, Red/White

Hook:	2/0.
Thread:	Red, size A.
Tail:	20 to 30 strands of silver Flashabou (3"). Two clumps of white bucktail.
Body:	5/8" balsawood. Shaped with jig support, or by hand. Cut slot for hook shank on bottom of balsa. Face is cupped and slanted. Wood is covered with sanding sealer. Color is applied with airbrush.
Optics:	Prizmatic tape eyes, coat with 5-minute epoxy.
Suggested Uses:	Inshore, rocky shore, kelp beds, freshwater.

Barracuda Fly

Hook:	2/0.
Thread:	Chartreuse or fluorescent green.
Tail:	Fluorescent chartreuse chenille braided with catus chenille.
Skirt and Underbody:	Synthetic dubbing, Polar-Aire flourescent chartreuse.
Overbody:	Pearl Mylar tubing, extending past hook and picked out.
Optics:	Yellow/black pupil, hollow plastic doll eyes. Coat eyes and Mylar tubing with 5-minute epoxy.
Suggested Uses:	Estuary and flats.

Bass Popper

Hook:	4 or 6.
Thread:	Brown.
Tail:	Hackle, 3 per side. Topping, yellow marabou.
Skirt:	Grizzy, or fiery brown hackle.
Body:	Balsawood, shaped with jig support, or by hand. Paint applied with airbrush.
Optics:	Plastic doll eyes, small or medium.
Legs:	Rubber hackle, brown-white-tan.
Suggested Uses:	Freshwater and estuary.

Beadle Blue-Water Deceiver

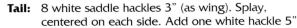

Hook: 4/0 to 7/0. (Use of a tandem hook design is recommended for offshore use. The rear hook should ride point up. All materials are tied on the forward hook.)

Thread: White.

Tail: White bucktail. 8 white saddle hackles per side. 2 magenta-dyed grizzly per side.

Body: White bucktail mixed with Flashabou, pearl and silver.

Wing: Magenta bucktail on top. Mixed with Krystal Flash, purple and pink. Add white bucktail below the shank. Repeat this combination of magenta on top and white below, two more times.

Cheeks: Red Flashabou or Krystal Flash.

Head and Optics: Tying thread creates the head. Color the top half with a marking pen. Add large (10mm) oval plastic doll eyes, hollow. Coat the entire head/eye construction with 5-minute epoxy.

Suggested Uses: Offshore and inshore.

Blanton's Sar-Mul-Mac

Hook: 1/0-4/0.

Thread: Size A, white.

Tail: White bucktail, medium bunch, length 4".

Hackle Wing: 6 to 9 white saddle hackles.

Wing Flash: 6 to 8 silver Mylar strips, shorter than hackle.

Overwing: Blue bucktail, green flash.

Collar: Red chenille, medium, two turns.

Head Topping: 12 strands of peacock herl.

Optics: 4 to 8mm glass eyes, amber.

Head: White chenille.

Suggested Uses: Inshore, offshore, estuary.

Blanton's Sea Arrow Squid

Hook: 2/0-4/0.

Thread: White, size A.

Tip: Gold Mylar.

Butt: Large white chenille wrapped into a ball.

Tail: 8 white saddle hackles 3" (as wing). Splay, centered on each side. Add one white hackle 5" long to each side. Add a few strands of coarse purple bucktail (3") and purple Krystal Flash to each side.

Optics: 8mm glass eyes, amber.

Topping and Throat: Fill the gap between the eyes with white marabou.

Body: Build the base with floss or cotton. Taper it toward the hook eye. Wrap with medium chenille, white. Leave room near hook eye to add two tufts of calf tail as a posterior fin.

Suggested Uses: Inshore, offshore, kelp beds.

Blanton's Tropical Punch

Hook: 2/0-3/0.

Thread: Hot orange, size A.

Optics: Large silver bead chain.

Tail: Medium bunch of yellow bucktail.

Tail Flash: 25 to 30 strands of gold Flashabou per side.

Body: Gold Mylar.

Hackle: Yellow saddle hackle, large webbed.

Topping: Layered. Yellow Krystal Hair, peacock Krystal Hair, peacock herl 10 to 15 strands.

Wing: Hot orange grizzly saddle hackle to length of tail, one per side.

Head: Medium chenille, hot orange. Topped with overlay of peacock herl.

Suggested Uses: Inshore, estuary, rocky shore, kelp beds.

Chico Bonefish Special

Hook: 2.

Thread: Black.

Tail: Orange marabou.

Underbody: Flat gold Mylar.

Overbody: Clear monfilament.

Wing: White bucktail, sparse. Two grizzly hackles.

Suggested Uses: Estuary and flats.

Cockroach

Hook: 3/0-4/0.
Thread: Black.
Wing: 6 to 8 strands of Krystal Flash, pearl. Four grizzly hackles per side.
Collar: Natural brown squirrel tail.
Head/Beak: Black thread.
Optics: Small plastic doll eyes, or prizmatic tape eyes.
Suggested Uses: Estuary and flats.

Crazy Charlie, crystal brown

Hook: 4-8.
Thread: Tan or white.
Optics: Small bead chain, gold.
Tail: Krystal Flash, pink.
Body and Overwrap: Flat tinsel, silver. Clear V-rib.
Wing: Krystal Flash, pink. Two brown hackle tips.
Suggested Uses: Estuary and flats.

Crazy Charlie, crystal chartreuse

Hook: 4-8.
Thread: Chartreuse or white.
Optics: Small bead chain, gold.
Tail: Krystal Flash, fluorescent chartreuse.
Body and Overwrap: Tying thread. Clear V-rib.
Wing: Krystal Flash, fluorescent chartreuse. Two chartreuse dyed grizzly tips.
Suggested Uses: Estuary and flats.

Crazy Charlie, silver

Hook: 4-8.
Thread: White.
Optics: Small bead chain, silver.
Tail: Pearl Flashabou.
Body and Overwrap: Flat tinsel, silver. Clear V-rib.
Wing: Two white hackle tips.
Suggested Uses: Estuary and flats.

Crystal Popper

Hook: 2/0.
Thread: Red, size A.
Body: 5/8" balsawood. Shaped with jig support, or by hand. Cut slot for hook shank on bottom of balsa. Face is cupped and slanted. Wood is covered with sanding sealer Color is applied with airbrush.
Optics: Prizmatic tape eyes.
Overbody and Tail: Pearl Mylar tubing. Pulled over painted body, extending two inches past hook to create tail. Apply 5-minute epoxy as coating on body only.
Suggested Uses: Inshore, rocky shore, kelp beds.

Dahlberg Saltwater Diver

Hook: 1/0.
Thread: White size A, or 3/0.
Tail: Rabbit strip, white. 6 to 8 strands Pearl Flashabou per side.
Collar: Deer hair, red.
Head: Deer hair, red and white.
Optics: Yellow/black pupil, solid plastic doll eyes, 4-1/2mm.
Suggested Uses: Inshore, estuary, flats.

Del's Permit Fly

Hook: #2.
Thread: Chartreuse or fluorescent green.
Claws: Flashabou, sparse, pearl. 4 ginger variant hackle tips per side.
Legs: Rubber hackle, white. Tips tinted red with marker.
Body: Yarn, alternate strands of brown and tan.
Optics: Medium barbell eyes.
Suggested Uses: Estuary, flats, surf zone.

Fire-Bellied Newt

Hook: 4.
Thread: Brown.
Optics: Medium barbell eyes, painted orange/black.
Tail: 4 broad neck hackles, fiery brown.
Ribbing: Copper wire, medium.
Body and Head: Buggy Nymph dubbing, cinnamon.
Belly Feather: Saddle hackle, hot orange or red.
Legs: Marabou, rusty brown.
Suggested Uses: Freshwater.

Fire Tiger Popper

Hook: 2 or 6.
Thread: White.
Weedguard: Monofilament.
Tail: Marabou, green and black. Yellow Krystal Flash, 4 strands.
Belly: Deer Hair, orange.
Back and Sides: Deer Hair, green. Deer Hair, black.
Optics: Plastic doll eyes; medium, chartreuse and black.
Belly Sparkle: Ultrafine Pearlescent Glitter.
Suggested Uses: Freshwater.

Grass Shrimp

Hook: 2.
Thread: Gray.
Mouth: Bucktail, gray, small bunch. Krystal Flash, sparse, pearl.
Antenna: Stripped hackle stem, grizzly.
Optics: Plastic bead eyes.
Carapace: Bucktail, gray.
Body: Lite Brite, pearl, picked out.
Suggested Uses: Surf zone and estuary.

Green Machine

Hooks: Two, short shank, tied tandem so rear hook rides point up.
Tubing: 1/8" outside diameter, completely through the foam extending approx. 1". A second tube (1/4" OD) will be placed over the extension at the rear. Used ultimately to accept the front hook eye. A third tube (3/8" OD) will be used to tie on the wing, then slid over the second tubing.
Wing: White bucktail (5-6"). Flashabou, pearl. Fluorescent green bucktail, chartreuse Krystal Flash, fluorescent blue and green FisHair. 30 fluorescent green hackles create the bulk of the wing. Two blue hackles for accent on each side, with blue Krystal Flash.
Popper Head: Fluorescent green, stick on prism eyes.
Suggested Uses: Offshore.

Gurgler Fly

Hook: 2/0.
Thread: Fluorescent green.
Tail: 12 strands of pearl Flashabou. 3 olive-dyed grizzly hackles per side, splayed.
Body: Yellow, closed-cell foam, cut to shape.
Beard: Red synthetic, bristle brush.
Suggested Uses: Estuary and flats.

Hot Flash Minnow

Hook: 2-4.
Thread: Olive.
Body Support: Monofilament tied to create a loop extending one full length behind the shank.
Body: All material is tied in approximately 1/4 down the shank. White bucktail, sparse, 3" long. One olive hackle per side. Angel Hair, gold and green, used sparsely all around to add to the profile.
Topping: Olive dubbing.
Head: Tying thread.
Optics: Holographic solid plastic eyes, red/black pupil.
Suggested uses: Freshwater.

Lefty's Deceiver, blue/white

Hook: 2-4/0.
Thread: White.
Tail: 6 white saddle hackles. 6 to 12 pearl Krystal Flash per side.
Body: Flat tinsel, silver.
Wing: Bucktail, blue on top. White bucktail below.
Topping: Peacock herl, a few strands.
Hackle
Wing: One grizzly per side.
Throat: Red Krystal Flash.
Head and
Optics: Tying thread painted blue or black. Small plastic doll eyes, or painted eyes white/black pupil.
Suggested
Uses: Inshore, offshore, estuary, rocky shore, kelp beds, surf zone.

Lefty's Deceiver, green/white

Hook: 2-4/0.
Thread: Fluorescent green.
Tail: 6 white saddle hackles. 6 to 12 Pearl Krystal Flash per side.
Body: Flat tinsel, silver.
Wing: Bucktail, green on top. White bucktail below.
Topping: Peacock herl, a few strands.
Hackle
Wing: One grizzly per side.
Throat: Red Krystal Flash
Head and
Optics: Tying thread. Small plastic doll eyes, or painted eyes white/black pupil.
Suggested
Uses: Inshore, offshore, estuary, rocky shore.

Lefty's Deceiver, yellow/chartreuse

Hook: 2-4/0.
Thread: Chartreuse or fluorescent green.
Tail: 6 yellow saddle hackles. 6 to 12 gold Krystal Flash per side.
Body: Flat tinsel, gold.

Wing: Bucktail, chartreuse top and bottom.
Hackle
Wing: One yellow-dyed grizzly per side.
Head and
Optics: Tying thread. Small plastic doll eyes, or painted eyes silver/black pupil.
Suggested
Uses: Inshore, offshore, estuary, rocky shore.

Mini Puff, brown

Hook: 4.
Thread: Brown or tan.
Optics: Small bead chain.
Body: Pearl Mylar.
Wing: Brown calf tail. Two orange grizzly hackle tips.
Head: Brown chenille, small or medium.
Suggested
Uses: Estuary and flats.

Mini Puff, pink

Hook: 4.
Thread: Pink.
Optics: Small bead chain.
Body: Pearl Mylar.
Wing: Brown calf tail. Two grizzly hackle tips.
Head: Pink chenille, small or medium.
Suggested
Uses: Estuary and flats.

Rabbitron Crab

Hook: 2.
Thread: Olive.
Claws: Antron, olive-gray-white.
Roe Ball: Medium chenille, hot pink.
Body: Rabbit strip, orange and olive.
Suggested
uses: Surf zone, estuary, flats.

Red & White Tarpon

Hook: 3/0-4/0.
Thread: Red.
Wing: 6-8 strands Krystal Flash, silver. Four white hackles per side.
Collar: Red saddle hackle.
Head/Beak: Red thread.
Optics: Small plastic doll eyes, or prizmatic tape eyes.
Suggested Uses: Estuary, flats, inshore.

Surf Grub

Hook: #2.
Thread: Olive.
Tail: Antron, gray-olive-orange. Marabou, tan and gray.
Body: Antron, olive.
Optics: Small barbell eyes.
Head: Medium chenille, hot pink.
Suggested Uses: Surf zone, estuary, flats.

V-worm

Hook: #4.
Thread: Black.
Weedguard: Monofilament.
Tail: Vernille or Ultra Chenille (5").
Tip: Marabou, fluorescent green.
Body: Buggy Nymph dubbing, black.
Suggested Uses: Freshwater, rocky shore, kelp beds.

Specialty List of Angling Resources

FishAbout
PO Box 1679, Los Gatos, CA 95031
(Baja, Riviera, Yucatán & Caribbean regions)

Anglers Inn International
9051-C Siempre Viva Rd., Suite 15-500, San Diego, CA 92173
(Northwest, Riviera regions) Bass specialists.

Fishing International, Inc.
4775 Sonoma Highway, Santa Rosa, CA 95409
(Baja, Riviera, Southwest, Caribbean regions)

Meling Adventures
PO Box 189003-73, Coronado, CA 92178
(Baja, northern region) Trout specialists.

The Anglers Connection
1122 12th Street, Cody, WY 82414
(Caribbean Coast region)

Posada Del Sol
1201 US Hwy. One, Suite 210, North Palm Beach, FL 33408
(Caribbean Coast region)

Baja Anglers
15115 N. Airport Drive, Scottsdale, AZ 85260
(Baja, southern region)

Baja On The Fly
PO Box 81961, San Diego, CA 92138
(Baja, southern region)